CAMBRIDGE LATIN

NORTH AMERICAN EDITION

WORKSHEET MASTERS
UNIT 1

EILEEN EMMETT, CATHERINE HUDSPITH,
PAMELA PERKINS AND PAT STORY

EDITED BY ED PHINNEY

WORKING PARTY

Eileen Emmett:	Classics teacher at the Perse School for Girls, Cambridge
Catherine Hudspith:	Head of the Classics Department, Sir William Perkins's School, Chertsey
Pamela Perkins:	Head of the Classics Department, City of London School for Girls
Pat Story:	Director of the Cambridge School Classics Project and Latin teacher at Coleridge Community College, Cambridge

EDITOR

Ed Phinney: University of Massachusetts at Amherst

Published by the Press Syndicate of the University of Cambridge
The Pitt Building, Trumpington Street, Cambridge CB2 1RP
40 West 20th Street, New York, NY10011–4211, USA
10 Stamford Road, Oakleigh, Melbourne 3166, Australia

© SCAA Enterprises Ltd 1995

COPYRIGHT

Because of the special nature of this publication, the publisher is waiving normal copyright provisions to the extent that copies of worksheets may be made free of charge and with specific permission so long as they are for educational or personal use within the school or institution which purchases the book. All other forms of copying (for example, for inclusion in another publication) are subject to specific permission from the publisher in the normal way.

First published 1995

Printed in Great Britain by Scotprint Ltd, Musselburgh

ISBN 0 521 45846 3

Preface

The worksheets in this book are designed to be used in conjunction with Unit 1 of the *Cambridge Latin Course*. The following types of exercise are provided for each Stage in the Unit:
- exercises consolidating Latin vocabulary, accidence and syntax;
- language awareness exercises, mainly involving work on Latin derivations in English and other modern languages;
- exercises testing aural comprehension;
- exercises extending and testing knowledge of Roman background.

Detailed information about the exercises and suggestions for their use are given in the Teacher's Notes at the end of this book.

In compiling the worksheets our task would have been much more onerous if we had not been able to draw on the expertise of many other classicists. Their generous help is acknowledged in detail below, but we should particularly like to record our special debt to Ed Phinney and Patricia Bell, editors of the North American *Cambridge Latin Course* Workbooks, whose work stimulated us to produce these worksheets, and to the North American Cambridge School Classics Project for allowing us to use or adapt several exercises from the Workbook for Unit 1.

We should also like to thank Richard Woff for his helpful suggestions and the following teachers and students for trying out the worksheets in school and commenting on their effectiveness: Lynda Goss and students at Codsall High School, Wolverhampton; Diana Sparkes and students at Cantell School, Southampton; and our own students at Clarendon School, Bedford; Sir William Perkins's School, Chertsey; the City of London School for Girls and Coleridge Community College, Cambridge.

We are grateful to Ian Johnstone of the Cambridge University Press for suggestions about the design of the worksheets, to Patricia Acres, Betty Munday and Margaret Widdess of the Project team for editorial assistance and to Maire Collins, the Project Secretary, for setting the text with her customary combination of flair and precision.

Eileen Emmett
Catherine Hudspith
Pamela Perkins
Pat Story

Acknowledgments

We thank the following for their permission to make use of their exercises:

North American Cambridge School Classics Project: 1.1; 2.1; 2.2; 2.3; 3.1; 3.5; 4.5; 5.4; 7.1; 7.5; 7.6; 9.3; 12.3

Marianne Schmid Lorinchak: 1.2

Adrian Spooner: 1.3; 4.4; 5.3; 6.1; 8.1

Patricia Kitto: 2.5

The Waterloo County Board of Education, Ontario: 3.4

The Minnesota Council on Quality Education: 4.1; 4.2; 4.3

Mark Woodward: 5.2

Helen Vicat: 6.3; 7.3

Richard Woff: 7.2

Verla Hall: 8.3

Pictures were drawn by Pamela Perkins for 2.4; 2.7; 5.7; 6.5; 8.7; 10.4; 12.6; by Helen Vicat for 8.4; 12.4; 12.7.

The picture in 7.7 is reproduced by kind permission of Dick Marshall.

1.1 What does he say? What does he do?

Find the answer to each question by filling the blanks with Latin words which translate the English. Then read the boxed letters downwards.

1 What does Grumio say?

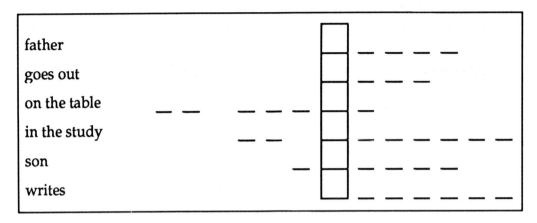

2 What does Cerberus do?

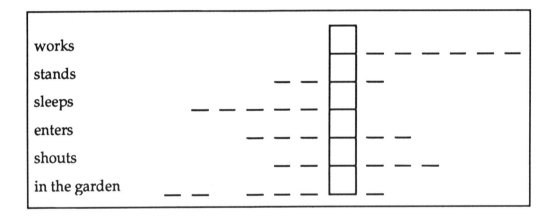

1.2 Where in the house?

You will hear a series of sentences. Decide where the person, animal or object is most likely to be. Mark the answer.

1 a) in viā   b) in tablīnō   c) in triclīniō
2 a) in culīnā   b) in viā   c) in tablīnō
3 a) in viā   b) in cubiculō   c) in ātriō
4 a) in hortō   b) in lātrīnā   c) in impluviō
5 a) in lātrīnā   b) in viā   c) in impluviō
6 a) in viā   b) in ātriō   c) in triclīniō
7 a) in ātriō   b) in viā   c) in mēnsā
8 a) in ātriō   b) in cubiculō   c) in mēnsā

© SCAA Enterprises Ltd

1.3 What's in a name?

1. You know that names have a meaning. Below you will find some names which come to us from the Latin language. Say what you think the name might mean. You may be given a word clue in brackets.

Victor/Victoria	_____	Rex (regal)	_____
Justin/Justine	_____	Gemma	_____
Flora	_____	Dominic (dominate)	_____
Gloria	_____	Leo/Leonie	_____
Stella (constellation)	_____	Max (maximum)	_____
Hilary	_____	Chris/Christine	_____

2. It may surprise you to discover what some Latin names mean. Match the names in the left-hand column with a Latin word and its meaning in the column on the right. Put the appropriate letter next to the name.

    i) Clēmēns   a) quīntus (fifth)
    ii) Jūlius   b) Iovilius (descended from Jove)
    iii) Caesar   c) clēmentia (mercy)
    iv) Claudius   d) fēlīcitās (luck)
    v) Quīntus   e) claudus (lame, limping)
    vi) Fēlīx   f) caesariēs (head of hair)

3. Some of our surnames have meanings which relate to a job or profession or skill, for example, Cook. Try to think of more surnames of this type.

    _____   _____   _____

    _____   _____   _____

    _____   _____   _____

1.4 in vīllā

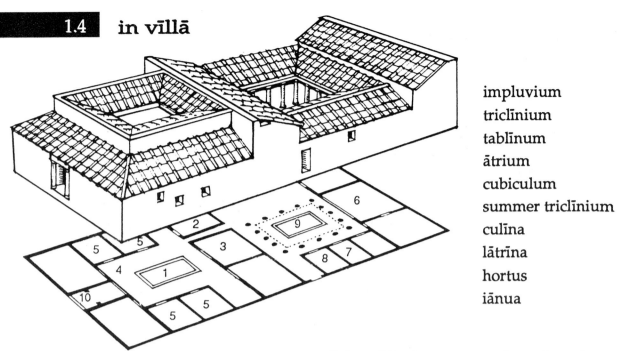

impluvium
triclīnium
tablīnum
ātrium
cubiculum
summer triclīnium
culīna
lātrīna
hortus
iānua

Fill in the spaces below with the correct English and Latin names, and numbers from the groundplan. Use the clues to help you.

English	Clues	Latin	Number
dining room	Three couches here. Clue: *triplet, trio, tricycle*	_____	2
hall	The first big room you enter	_____	—
garden	For people interested in *horticulture*	_____	—
door	A *janitor* might sit on duty here	_____	—
rainwater pool	French clue: *il pleut*	_____	—
_____	Very small room, not used much by day	cubiculum	—
_____	A *table* would be necessary here	tablīnum	3
_____	Sometimes called *latrine* today	lātrīna	8
_____	Near the lātrīna. Grumio's workplace	culīna	—
summer _____	A pleasant place to eat in the summer	summer _____	—

© SCAA Enterprises Ltd

2.1 Which answers are possible?

1. What does Metella taste? *Mark things Metella would enjoy tasting:*
   canem   culīnam   pecūniam   cēnam   hortum   pāvōnem   coquum

2. Whom does Clemens greet? *Mark only people:*
   amīcum   mēnsam   vīllam   mercātōrem   Quīntum   hortum   servum   ancillam   pāvōnem

3. Which rooms does Cerberus enter? *Mark only rooms:*
   ātrium   tablīnum   impluvium   cibum   triclīnium   culīnam   lectum   ancillam   vīnum   cubiculum

4. What does Metella do? *Mark actions appropriate for Metella:*
   salit   dormit   sedet   clāmat   vīsitat   cēnat   stertit   gustat

5. Whom does Metella hear? *Mark only animals or people:*
   fīlium   hortum   mēnsam   canem   coquum   pāvōnem   cēnam   ancillam

6. What does Caecilius do? *Mark actions appropriate for Caecilius:*
   scrībit   sedet   pecūniam numerat   lātrat   in lectō recumbit   salit   cantat   coquit

2.2 Find the hidden sentence

1. In this group, cross out every word describing a **person**. *Translate the sentence that remains:*
   māter   coquus   canis   fīlius   servus   pater   argentārius   in impluviō   ancilla   dominus   stat

   Translation: _____

2. In this group, cross out every word describing **movement**. *Translate the sentence that remains:*
   salit   pater   surgit   exit   coquum   portat   vīsitat   vituperat   intrat

   Translation: _____

3. In this group, cross out every **accusative case**. *Translate the sentence that remains:*
   cibum   culīnam   canis   amīcum   servum   pāvōnem   ancillam   mercātōrem   est   pecūniam   pestis   iānuam   fīlium

   Translation: _____

2.3 Cerberus

1 *Fill in the missing Latin word which matches the English or the picture. You will not use all the items in the lists.*

Nominative	Accusative	Verbs
Caecilius	Caecilium	clāmat
canis	canem	est
cēna	cēnam	exit
Cerberus	Cerberum	gustat
coquus	coquum	intrat
culīna	culīnam	laudat
dominus	dominum	parat
Grumiō	Grumiōnem	salūtat
servus	servum	stat

_____ est in culīnā. coquus _____
                                                    (dinner)

parat. Caecilius culīnam _____ . _____ cibum
                          (enters)   (The master)

gustat. Caecilius _____ laudat. Cerberus _____ intrat.
                   (the cook)   (the kitchen)

_____ cibum videt. _____ cibum gustat.
 (The dog)

Grumiō _____ videt. _____ nōn est laetus.
        (the dog)   (The slave)

'pestis!' _____ clāmat. _____ est
           (the cook)

īrātus. 'furcifer!' dominus_____ . Cerberus exit.
                            (shouts)

2 *Now translate the story.*

2.4 amīcus Grumiōnem vīsitat

Your job is to put the jumbled pictures in the right order. Listen to the story. Every time your teacher stops, number the picture which illustrates what has been read.

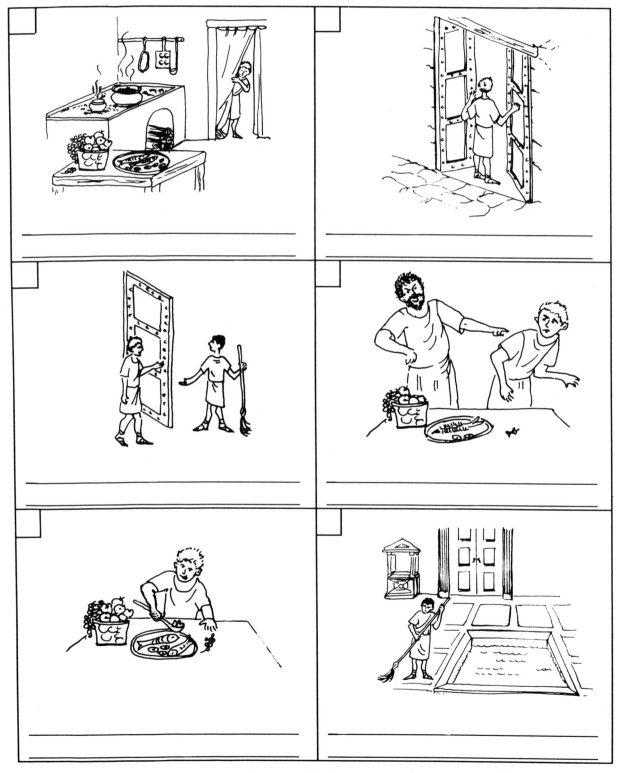

Now read the longer version of this story in Stage 2. Pick out a suitable Latin sentence for each picture and write this on the lines provided.

2.5 Using Latin

Using your knowledge of Latin, complete the following sentences by marking the correct answer.

1. A person uses culinary skills in
   a) flower arranging
   b) cooking
   c) cleaning

   Culinary comes from the Latin word _____

2. When animals are dormant they are
   a) attacking
   b) eating
   c) hibernating

   Dormant comes from the Latin word _____

3. A bibulous person likes
   a) the Bible
   b) drinking
   c) growing bulbs

   Bibulous comes from the Latin word _____

4. A cantata is
   a) sung
   b) danced
   c) recited

   Cantata comes from the Latin word _____

5. A recumbent person is
   a) standing to attention
   b) lying down
   c) running

   Recumbent comes from the Latin word _____

6. An impecunious person
   a) has no money
   b) is unintelligent
   c) is impolite

   Impecunious comes from the Latin word _____

7. The optimum number is
   a) the highest
   b) the lowest
   c) the best

   Optimum comes from the Latin word _____

© SCAA Enterprises Ltd

2.6 Roman dinner parties

Here are some real Roman dishes and two descriptions of meals by Roman writers.

gustātiō	*prīmae mēnsae*	*secundae mēnsae*
Starters	Main dishes	Desserts
Leeks with olives	Stuffed hare with white sauce, dried peas and leeks	Dates stuffed with nuts and pine kernels fried in honey
Snails fried in oil, garum and pepper	Fallow deer roasted with onion sauce, Jericho dates, raisins, oil and honey	Pastry cases filled with honey and walnuts
Sows' udders stuffed with salted sea-urchins	Dormice stuffed with pork and pine kernels	Milk and egg sweet
Mussels in sweet wine sauce	Ham boiled with figs and baked in pastry with honey	Fresh fruit - pomegranates, apples, grapes, plums
Boiled tree fungi with peppered garum sauce	Boiled chicken with dill sauce, cabbage and green lentils	

Mulsum - wine mixed with honey

Martial invites a friend to dinner.

You'll have a nice meal, Julius, at my house; do come if you've nothing better to do. Keep the eighth hour (two o'clock) free; we'll go to Stephanus' baths beforehand, just next door. For starters, you'll get lettuce, fresh young leeks, then salted tunny fish a little bigger than a mackerel and garnished with eggs done up with rue; then more eggs, this time baked to a turn in a moderate oven with cheese and olives. For the main course, you can have fish and oysters, sow-belly, chicken and duck. I promise I won't recite anything, but you can read me your poem *The Giants* again, or recite some of the ones about the countryside.

Pliny complains about a guest who failed to turn up.

What do you mean by accepting my invitation to dinner and then not turning up? It was all set out, a lettuce each, three snails, two eggs, barley-water, wine with honey, chilled with snow (an expensive item, please note, since it disappears in the dish!), some olives, beetroots, gherkins, onions and plenty of other delicacies as well. You could have had a comic play, a poetry reading or a singer. But no, instead you preferred to go where you could have oysters, sows' innards, sea urchins and Spanish dancing girls!

Design an invitation to a cēna, a Roman dinner party, using Roman names and referring to Roman customs. Select your menu (including drinks) and describe the entertainments.

© SCAA Enterprises Ltd

2.7 More about Roman food

Ordinary Romans did not eat much meat. Their main food was wheat flour, which was made into bread or porridge. They added herbs, vegetables and other flavourings to make their simple diet more interesting.

Wealthy people had a more varied menu and ate much more meat and fish. A favourite sauce was the strong, salty *garum*, made from fish entrails. At a *cēna* people might eat as many as seven courses.

1. There is one food in each group which the Romans did **not** eat. Circle it and pick out from the word the letter indicated in the column on the right. Re-arrange the letters to complete the sentence below.

   a) potatoes   cabbage   onions   olives   2nd letter   __
   b) chicken   lamb   curry   mushrooms   5th letter   __
   c) figs   raisins   chocolate   pears   2nd letter   __
   d) cherries   bananas   dates   walnuts   3rd letter   __
   e) tea   wine   olive-oil   fish-sauce   2nd letter   __

   The Romans relied on __ __ __ __ __ as a sweetener

2. Spot the differences. There are five things missing in one of these pictures of a *cēna*.

© SCAA Enterprises Ltd

3.1 How are these words connected?

Each of the Latin words in the box is connected with an English word in the list below. Match up the English and Latin words. Then show what their connection is. Use a dictionary to help you if necessary. The first one is done for you.

stat	canis	portat	dormit	clāmat
vīnum	māter	audit	dominus	laudat

	English	Latin	Connection
1	stationary	stat	stationary (standing still) stat (stands)
2	maternal	_____	_____
3	laudable	_____	_____
4	audience	_____	_____
5	clamor	_____	_____
6	canine	_____	_____
7	dominate	_____	_____
8	vinegar	_____	_____
9	porter	_____	_____
10	dormitory	_____	_____

3.2 True or false?

Your teacher will read four sentences about each picture. Decide whether each statement is true or false and write the answers (T or F) underneath the picture.

 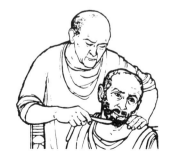 

A 1__ 2__ 3__ 4__   B 1__ 2__ 3__ 4__   C 1__ 2__ 3__ 4__

© SCAA Enterprises Ltd

3.3 Celer, Pantagathus, Syphāx

Here are some words taken from the stories in this Stage and pictures of the main characters in the stories. Write beside the pictures the words that are connected with each character and give their meaning.

tondet	vēnālīcius	leō	nāvis	pictūra
secat	triclīnium	pingit	taberna	servus
emit	tōnsor	novācula	pictor	ancilla

Celer

Latin word | Meaning
1 _____ | _____
2 _____ | _____
3 _____ | _____
4 _____ | _____
5 _____ | _____

Pantagathus

Latin word | Meaning
1 _____ | _____
2 _____ | _____
3 _____ | _____
4 _____ | _____
5 _____ | _____

Syphāx

Latin word | Meaning
1 _____ | _____
2 _____ | _____
3 _____ | _____
4 _____ | _____
5 _____ | _____

© SCAA Enterprises Ltd

3.4 Who's who?

*Read each sentence. Then replace the name in **bold** letters by a word which shows the person's job or position. Use the words in the box below, making sure you have chosen the correct case. By the end you should have used each word once.*

ancilla	ancillam	māter	mātrem
pictor	pictōrem	argentārius	argentārium
coquus	coquum	servus	servum
tōnsor	tōnsōrem	vēnālīcius	vēnālīcium

For example: **Clēmēns** vīnum portat.   vēnālīcius **Melissam** laudat.

servus vīnum portat.   vēnālīcius *ancillam* laudat.

1 **Caecilius** pecūniam numerat.

   _____ pecūniam numerat.

2 amīcus **Caecilium** salūtat.

   amīcus _____ salūtat.

3 **Clēmēns** ātrium intrat.

   _____ ātrium intrat.

4 **Metella** cibum gustat.

   _____ cibum gustat.

5 dominus **Melissam** emit.

   dominus _____ emit.

6 **Celer** iānuam pulsat.

   _____ iānuam pulsat.

7 fīlius **Clēmentem** vocat.

   fīlius _____ vocat.

8 dominus **Grumiōnem** laudat.

   dominus _____ laudat.

9 **Pantagathus** barbam tondet.

   _____ barbam tondet.

10 **Grumiō** cēnam coquit.

   _____ cēnam coquit.

11 mercātor **Syphācem** quaerit.

   mercātor _____ quaerit.

12 canis **Celerem** audit.

   canis _____ audit.

13 **Melissa** linguam Latīnam discit.

   _____ linguam Latīnam discit.

14 canis **Metellam** spectat.

   canis _____ spectat.

15 senex **Pantagathum** vituperat.

   senex _____ vituperat.

16 **Syphāx** servum habet.

   _____ servum habet.

© SCAA Enterprises Ltd

3.5 Herculēs et leō

Stories about Hercules were very popular with the Greeks and Romans. One story told how he killed a fierce lion which lived in a cave near the Greek town of Nemea and terrorized the local people. Read the story below and then answer the questions.

Herculēs ad cavernam venit. hērōs leōnem quaerit. leō Herculem audit et fremit. leō ē cavernā venit et circumspectat. Herculēs nōn est perterritus. hērōs est fortis.

Herculēs sagittam conicit. sagitta leōnem pulsat sed pellem nōn
5   secat.

'ēheu!' inquit Herculēs.

leō salit et Herculem ferōciter petit. hērōs fūstem tenet et leōnem verberat. sed leō quoque est fortis. leō rīdet. hērōs est īrātus.

'pestis! furcifer!' clāmat Herculēs et leōnem strangulat.
10   hērōs est laetissimus.

Words and phrases

ad cavernam	to the cave	sagittam	arrow
hērōs	hero	conicit	shoots
fremit	roars	pellem	skin
		strangulat	strangles

	Points
1 What does Hercules do when he comes to the cave?	1
2 Why does the lion roar?	1
3 What does the lion do when it comes out of the cave?	1
4 Why is Hercules not afraid?	1
5 Which weapon does Hercules use first? Why do you think it fails?	2
6 How does Hercules feel at this point in the fight? Which Latin word tells you this?	2
7 Which weapon does Hercules try next?	1
8 *leō rīdet* (line 8). Why do you think the lion does this?	1
9 What does Hercules shout at the lion?	1
10 How does Hercules finally succeed in killing the lion?	1
	12

This was one of the twelve tasks which Hercules had to perform. They are known as the 'Labors of Hercules'. Do you know what the other labors were?

© SCAA Enterprises Ltd

3.6 In Pompeii

Match each of the letters on the plan of Pompeii with one of the clues given below.

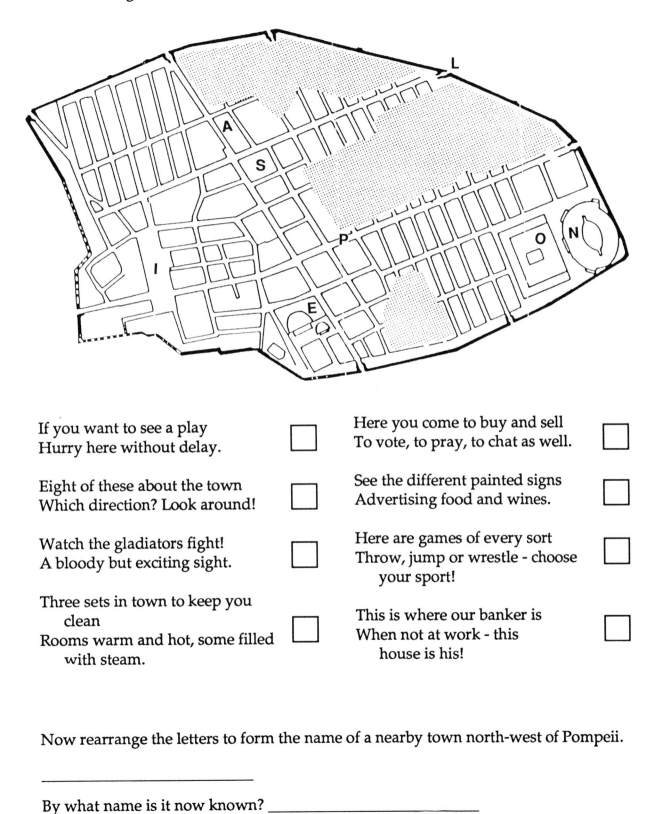

If you want to see a play
Hurry here without delay. ☐

Eight of these about the town
Which direction? Look around! ☐

Watch the gladiators fight!
A bloody but exciting sight. ☐

Three sets in town to keep you clean
Rooms warm and hot, some filled with steam. ☐

Here you come to buy and sell
To vote, to pray, to chat as well. ☐

See the different painted signs
Advertising food and wines. ☐

Here are games of every sort
Throw, jump or wrestle - choose your sport! ☐

This is where our banker is
When not at work - this house is his! ☐

Now rearrange the letters to form the name of a nearby town north-west of Pompeii.

_____

By what name is it now known? _____

© SCAA Enterprises Ltd

4.1 Who am I?

On the left you will see a series of sentences followed by the question 'quis sum ego?' Write down the answer on the right. The first one is done for you.

1. ego servum vēndō.
   quis sum ego?   tū es vēnālīcius!

2. ego pecūniam habeō.
   quis sum ego?   _____

3. ego barbam tondeō.
   quis sum ego?   _____

4. ego in ātriō sedeō.
   quis sum ego?   _____

5. ego in viā dormiō.
   quis sum ego?   _____

6. ego cēnam coquō.
   quis sum ego?   _____

7. ego leōnem pingō.
   quis sum ego?   _____

8. ego in triclīniō bibō.
   quis sum ego?   _____

9. ego in hortō labōrō.
   quis sum ego?   _____

10. ego linguam Latīnam discō.
    quis sum ego?   _____

Now make up some more examples of your own:

ego _____

quis sum ego?   tū _____

ego _____

quis sum ego?   tū _____

ego _____

quis sum ego?   tū _____

4.2 Links with Latin

Some European modern languages have words derived from Latin which look so much like the Latin that you can understand them. Match Latin words in the list below with their French, Italian and Spanish versions and write them in the box; then put the English meaning in the other box. You will not use all the Latin words in the list.

| ego respondeō | ego accūsō | ego dēbeō | ego portō | ego vēndō |
| tū respondēs | tū accūsās | tū dēbēs | tū portās | tū vēndis |

French, Italian, Spanish	Latin	English
French: j'accuse Italian: io accuso Spanish: yo acuso		
French: tu vends Italian: tu vendi Spanish: tu vendes		
French: tu réponds Italian: tu rispondi		
Italian: io devo Spanish: yo debo		
French: je porte Italian: io porto		

© SCAA Enterprises Ltd

4.3 A day in court

Here is a report of Hermogenes' trial with some of the details left out; fill in the gaps in English. You will find the answers in the play 'in basilicā'.

After the judge entered the _____ he asked Caecilius' name. Then he wanted to know if Caecilius was a _____ and what he did in the _____. Caecilius told the judge that he was a _____ and that he came to the _____ every day. He said that he was bringing a charge against _____ who owed him _____ and had not _____ it. Suddenly someone shouted that Caecilius was a _____. The judge did not like the interruption and asked '_____?' The man replied, '_____'. When the judge asked him what he was doing in the _____, he replied that he was a _____ and was doing business in the _____. Then the judge asked if he owed _____. Hermogenes replied that he _____ and that he had a friend who was a _____. Hermogenes' friend claimed that _____ did not _____ and that _____ was a liar. This made Caecilius so angry that he shouted out that _____ was a liar and so was his _____. The judge interrupted and said that Caecilius had to _____ his case. Caecilius said that he had a _____ and that the judge could _____ Hermogenes' _____ in the wax. _____ groaned and the judge asked him if he had a _____. Caecilius told the judge that Hermogenes was _____ his ring. The judge demanded the _____ and announced that it _____ the case. Then the _____ convicted Hermogenes.

© SCAA Enterprises Ltd

4.4 forum or basilica?

In this Stage you have learned about the business that was done in the forum and you have seen a trial in the basilica. Here are some words connected with either the forum or the basilica. Put them into their correct column below.

| taberna | testis | emit | tōnsor | rem nōn probat |
| iūdex | vēndit | accūsat | convincit | argentāria |

forum   basilica

1 _____   1 _____

2 _____   2 _____

3 _____   3 _____

4 _____   4 _____

5 _____   5 _____

4.5 How is Latin pronounced?

*Circle the English word that has the same (or almost the same) sound as the **bold** letters in the Latin words.*

1 f**i**lius

c**i**ty
ice
mater**i**al

2 la**e**tus

h**i**gh
l**a**y
n**ea**t

3 p**a**ter

m**a**ke
s**a**d
f**a**r

4 s**e**det

l**e**t
b**e**tween
n**ee**dle

5 c**u**līna

f**u**me
p**u**t
b**oo**t

6 Cae**c**ilius

simple
church
corner

7 re**dd**it

dew
rea**d**y
re**d d**oor

8 sur**g**it

gem
gag
soverei**g**n

9 implu**v**ium

violin
wonder
use

© SCAA Enterprises Ltd

4.6 Finding your way round the forum

Match up the letters in the picture with the clues below.

1. A good place to stroll in the heat of the day.
2. This way for the meeting hall of the cloth merchants.
3. Upright stones to stop wheeled traffic entering.
4. Easier to see and hear political speakers from here.
5. The ash from this will cover the *forum* completely.
6. This way for the *basilica*.
7. A famous citizen in the *forum*, but he's not alive.
8. The latest election result can be read from these boards.
9. The Temple of Jupiter stands at the north end.
10. Their togas tell you they are Roman citizens.
11. *amphorae* are large clay jars for storing wine or oil.
12. No carriages allowed? It doesn't matter if you can afford to be carried in a *lectica*.

Now work out the rest of this sentence.

        (1) (4)   (6) (2) (3) (8) (10)   (7) (5) (9) (12) (11)

Caecilius __ __ __ __ __ __ __ __ __ __ __ __

© SCAA Enterprises Ltd

5.1 Compliments or insults?

Would you be pleased if someone used the following words to describe you? Answer yes or no; give the meaning of the word and the Latin word from which it comes. Use an English dictionary to help you if necessary.

	Y/N	Meaning	Latin word
1 magnificent			
2 ridiculous			
3 servile			
4 mendacious			
5 responsive			
6 judicious			
7 egotistical			
8 circumspect			
9 tenacious			
10 scurrilous			

What do you notice about the endings of five of the English words on the left? Think of three other examples of describing words (adjectives) with the same ending.

_____   _____   _____

© SCAA Enterprises Ltd

5.2 Singular or plural?

Your teacher will read eight sentences in Latin. Each of them describes one of the pictures below. As you hear each sentence write the picture letter in the box next to the sentence number.

A
B
C
D
E
F
G
H

1. ☐ 2. ☐ 3. ☐ 4. ☐
5. ☐ 6. ☐ 7. ☐ 8. ☐

© SCAA Enterprises Ltd

5.3 Latin words in English

You now know the differences between the singular and plural forms of Latin words. Latin words that are used in English often form their plural in the Latin way. See if you can fill in the gaps below.

Singular	Plural
cactus	_____
_____	formulae
_____	narcissi
axis	_____
_____	radii
larva	_____
fungus	_____
_____	appendices
vertebra	_____
matrix	_____

The crocodiles call us hippopotamuses; we think _____ is more elegant.

5.4 Find the hidden sentence

1. *In this group of words cross out every **plural** word. Translate the sentence that remains.*

   mercātōrēs āctōrēs nūntius fēminae servī
   agricolae in forō nautae pāstōrēs clāmat

2. *In this group cross out every word relating to the **theater**. Translate the sentence that remains.*

   āctor scaena Pompēiānī plaudunt ad urbem
   spectat fābula theātrum contendunt spectātor

3. *In this group cross out every **plural** word. Translate the sentence that remains.*

   petunt labōrant senex spectant ambulant
   in theātrō plaudunt stant dormit sedent

4. *In this group cross out every word relating to **sound**. Translate the sentence that remains.*

   audit servus clāmor in vīllā plaudit
   cantant lātrat vocant manet recitat

© SCAA Enterprises Ltd

5.5 in theātrō

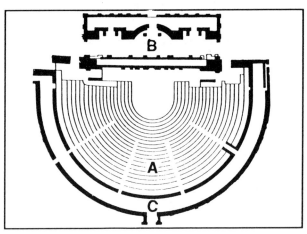

1. *Write the appropriate letter from the plan in the box next to the correct sentence.*

   ☐ Pompēiānī theātrum intrant.

   ☐ āctōrēs fābulam agunt.

   ☐ spectātōrēs fābulam exspectant.

2. *Mark the correct answer to complete the sentence.*

   Town councillors had seats:
   a) at the back
   b) at the front

   Seats were made of:
   a) wood
   b) stone

   The cost of admission:
   a) varied
   b) was free

   Plays began:
   a) early in the morning
   b) at midday

   Between plays attendants:
   a) sprinkled scented water
   b) made offerings to the gods

   The large theater was provided with:
   a) a roof
   b) a canvas awning

   Tickets were made of:
   a) bone
   b) silver

   Expenses were paid by:
   a) the town council
   b) a wealthy citizen

   Plays were put on:
   a) several times a year
   b) every market day

   On the day of a performance:
   a) shops were closed
   b) business increased

3. *Underline the word which would NOT apply to the spectators.*

SEDENT	PLAUDUNT	SPECTANT
14 7 15	13 12	8 11 9 3

LABŌRANT	CLĀMANT	AUDIUNT
4 5	2 16 10	1 6 17

   Rearrange the letters in the order indicated above to form a Latin sentence. Put X on the plan above where this would happen and translate the sentence.

   __ __ __   __ __ __ __ __ __ __

   __ __ __ __

© SCAA Enterprises Ltd

5.6 The Ghost

The following scene is taken from a comedy called The Ghost, *written by the Roman playwright, Plautus. In the play a young man is having a good time while his father is abroad. One day he is having a party in front of his house when his slave Tranio arrives with the news that his father has returned unexpectedly. The young man panics, but Tranio hustles everyone into the house, locks the door and hides. The father comes on to the stage and walks up to the door.*

Father What's this? The door locked in broad daylight! *(knocks loudly)* Hello, is anyone in? Open the door will you?

Tranio Who's this at our door?

F Why, it's my slave Tranio!

T Hello, master. I'm glad to see you're back safely.

F What's the matter with you? Are you crazy?

T What do you mean?

F I mean that you are wandering about outside, there's no one inside to unlock the door and no one to answer it. I've nearly broken down the door with my knocking.

T You didn't touch the door, did you?

F Of course I touched it! I battered it!

T Oh no!

F What's the matter?

T Something terrible!

F What do you mean?

T It's too awful to talk about - the dreadful thing you've done!

F What?

T Run! get away from the house! run!

F For heaven's sake, tell me what's the matter!

T No one has set foot in this house for the last seven months, ever since we moved out.

F Why's that? Tell me straight!

T Take a look around; see if there's anyone who can hear us.

F There's no one. Out with it!

T A dreadful crime was committed.

F What sort of crime? Who committed it? Tell me.

T The man who sold you the house murdered a guest here.

F Murdered him?

T And stole his money and buried him - here in the house!

F What makes you suspect this?

T I'll tell you. Listen. One night after your son came back from a dinner party, we all went to bed and fell asleep. And then, suddenly, he gave out a yell!

F Who did? My son?

T Sh-h-h. Keep quiet. Just listen. He said that the dead man came to him in a dream and said *(dramatically)* 'I am Diapontius, a stranger from over the sea. I haunt this house; I cannot enter the Underworld because I died before my time. My host murdered me for my money and buried me in this house secretly and without a proper funeral. Go from this place now. This house is accursed.' *(There is a noise inside the house)*

F *(terrified)* Sh-h-h!

T Good heavens! What was that?

F The door creaked!

T *(aside)* I'm done for. Those fools inside will ruin me and my story.

F What's that you're saying?

T Get away from the door! Run, for heaven's sake!

F Run where? You run with me!

T I have nothing to fear. I am at peace with the dead.

Voice inside: Hey Tranio!

T You won't call me, if you've any sense. I didn't knock on the door!

F Who are you talking to, Tranio?

T *(in surprise)* Was it you that called me? I thought the ghost was getting angry because you knocked on the door. Why are you still standing here? Get away as fast as you can and pray to Hercules.

F Hercules, I pray to thee! *(runs away)*

T And so do I - to bring this old chap the worst of luck.

© SCAA Enterprises Ltd

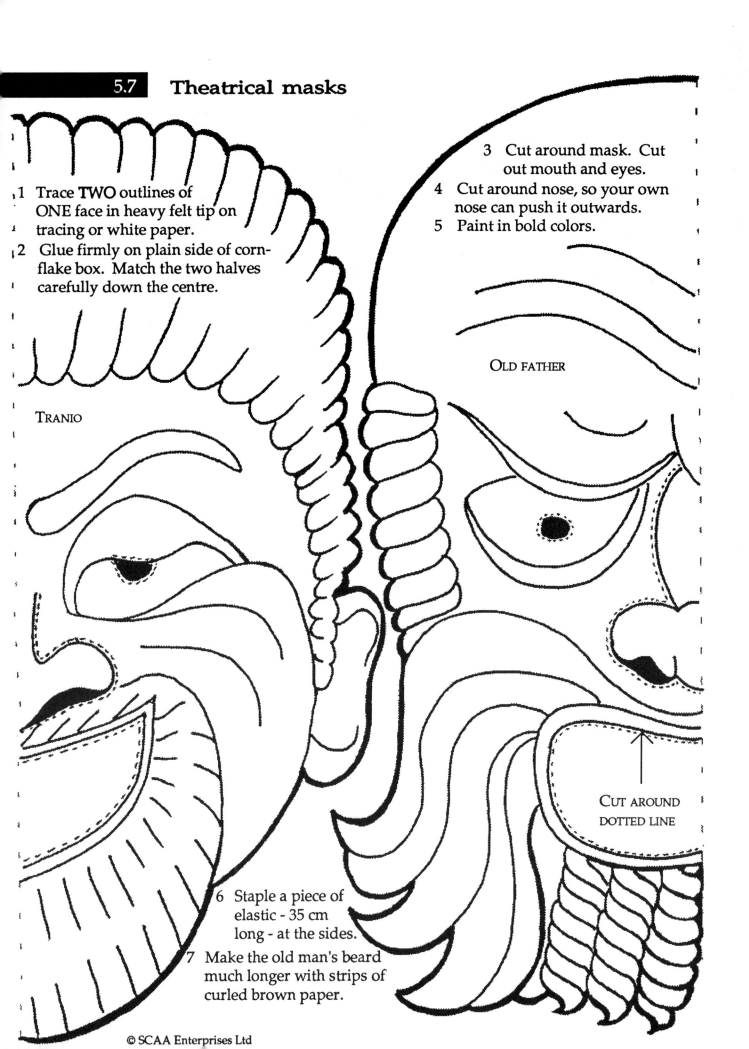

6.1 pugna

You have met the following words which have some connection with fighting. Choose **FIVE** of them and give an English derivation from them. Show that you know what the English word means by including it in a sentence of your own. Use a dictionary to help you if necessary.

pugna fortis superāvit clāmor pulsāvit īrātus incitābant vexābat

	Word	Derivation	Sentence
1	_____	_____	_____
2	_____	_____	_____
3	_____	_____	_____
4	_____	_____	_____
5	_____	_____	_____

6.2 After or because?

Complete each sentence with the most suitable group of words below.

postquam fābulam spectāvērunt	quod cēna erat optima
quod dominus dormiēbat	postquam ānulum spectāvit
postquam tabernam intrāvit	quod erant īrātī

1 amīcī, _____, coquum laudābant.
2 agricolae, _____, mercātōrem pulsābant.
3 iūdex, _____, Hermogenem vituperāvit.
4 Pompēiānī, _____, āctōrēs laudāvērunt.
5 Caecilius, _____, vīnum gustāvit.
6 servus, _____, nōn labōrābat.

6.3 poēta et canis

Translate the story into English.

1. Fēlīx et amīcī in tabernā bibēbant. poēta intrāvit.

2. amīcī poētam spectābant; poēta cantābat. amīcī nōn erant contentī. 'satis! satis!' clāmāvērunt.

3. subitō Fēlīx ē tabernā festīnāvit. lībertus canem quaesīvit.

4. Fēlīx canem in tabernam portāvit, ubi poēta cantābat.

5. canis poētam audīvit, et ferōciter lātrāvit.

6. omnēs amīcī rīdēbant; paene lacrimābant. poēta īrātus ē tabernā festīnāvit.

7. Fēlīx et amīcī canem laudāvērunt. canis erat laetissimus.

© SCAA Enterprises Ltd

6.4 What did they do?

Your teacher will read a sentence to you with the last word missed out. Underline the form of the word which would complete the sentence correctly and translate the whole sentence. The first four have pictures to help you.

1

numerāvit/numerāvērunt

2

ambulābat/ambulābant

3

sedēbat/sedēbant

4

vēndēbat/vēndēbant

5 recitāvit/recitāvērunt   6 pulsāvit/pulsāvērunt
7 labōrābat/labōrābant   8 festīnāvit/festīnāvērunt

Translation:

1 _____
2 _____
3 _____
4 _____
5 _____
6 _____
7 _____
8 _____

© SCAA Enterprises Ltd

6.5 The life of a slave

You are a slave at an auction in the forum in Pompeii. Slaves of all ages and nationalities stand there, and imported ones have their feet marked with chalk. They wear placards telling buyers their details.

Rules:

Make a paper token to move round the board. Toss a coin to move.
Heads: move to the black semi-circle.
Tails: move to the white. Write down what happens to you. What does your placard say? Toss a coin and find out…

START

'Italian, about 10 years. Abandoned at birth. No longer needed on farm.'

'Greek female, 20 years. Sold into slavery to pay husband's debts. Healthy.'

You are sold to an ambitious young writer who admires Greek literature, to give readings at his parties.

He is kind to you and you serve him loyally for 10 years. He frees you in order to marry you.

He cannot afford to keep up costly entertainments. He sells you.

You are sold to a rich business man to nurse his children.

You are let off work to bear home-born slaves who will be trained as secretaries, accountants and readers.

When your master dies you are set free and become a *liberta* under the terms of his will.

You run away but are recaptured and forced to wear a slave tag.

The land owner dies. His son inherits the lands, tools and slaves. He puts you on skilled work, tending vines.

You are sent to a huge estate in southern Italy. You are chained at night and cruelly over-worked.

You are bought by a freedman to help in his new bakery in Pompeii.

Your master is moody, but life in a town is easier. In the end you are put in charge of two other slaves.

You work well and your master rewards you at 30 by freeing you in the manumission ceremony.

Using the results of the game, write an account of your life, or give an interview about your life, or act out a scene in the slave auction.

© SCAA Enterprises Ltd

7.1 What do you see in the picture?

First study the picture and then circle the names of all the objects and persons that are pictured, either whole or in part.

amīcus	leō
Caecilius	turba
cibus	mēnsa
cubiculum	pōculum
hortus	cēna
lectus	triclīnium
barba	canis

7.2 fābula mīrābilis

Look at the picture. Your teacher will read five sentences about it. As you hear each sentence, write its letter in the correct box.

© SCAA Enterprises Ltd

7.3 The wasp

Translate the sentences below into English.

1. dominus vespam audīvit. vespam timēbat.

2. dominus servum cōnspexit. servum vocāvit.

3. servus vespam agitābat. vespam pulsāvit.

4. vespa īrāta erat. servum vulnerāvit.

5. servus clāmābat. vespam vituperāvit.

6. ancilla clāmōrem audīvit. vespam necāvit et servum servāvit.

Words and phrases

vespam	a wasp	vulnerāvit	wounded

7.4 Night horror

1. *In the story below, there are many words which come almost directly from Latin. Pick out these words and write them beside the Latin ones below.*

In an agricultural area of Italy, it was a cold, dark night and the moon was obscured by clouds. All the nocturnal animals were awake and made such a noise that they were driving the local inhabitants insane. Suddenly there came a terrifying howl, which filled everyone with horror. One solitary man was brave enough to venture out cautiously into the now deserted outskirts of the village. All was silent except for the rustle of the bushes. He feared that he might be in mortal danger, but knew his quest was vital. Again the bushes rustled and his pulse beat even faster. Would a terrible apparition rise up in front of him? He felt something brush against his leg – only to realize that the source of his terror was nothing more horrible than a black cat on the prowl.

Latin word	Word in the story	Latin word	Word in the story
appāret	*_____	obscūrus	*_____
terret	_____	vīta	*_____
cautē	_____	agricola	*_____
mortuus	*_____	nox, noctem	*_____
sōlus	*_____	horribilis	_____
dēsertus	_____	habitat	*_____
pulsat	_____	īnsānus	_____

2. *Choose **SIX** of the words marked with an asterisk and use each of them in an English sentence.*

a) _____

b) _____

c) _____

d) _____

e) _____

f) _____

7.5 Present or past?

In each Latin sentence, circle the word in the brackets which correctly translates the English word or words in bold type. Then put a mark in one of the boxes to indicate whether the sentence is in present or past time.

	Present	Past

1. Grumio **is preparing** the dinner.
   Grumiō cēnam (parāvit/parat).

2. The spectators **departed**.
   spectātōrēs (discessērunt/discēdunt).

3. The thief **makes for** the bedroom.
   fūr cubiculum (petit/petīvit).

4. Melissa **praised** the actor.
   Melissa āctōrem (laudat/laudāvit).

5. The dogs **frightened** the boy.
   canēs puerum (terruērunt/terrent).

6. The old men **heard** the racket.
   senēs clāmōrem (audīvērunt/audiunt).

7. The slaves **caught sight of** Decens.
   servī Decentem (cōnspiciunt/cōnspexērunt).

8. Grumio and Clemens **found fault with** Melissa.
   Grumiō et Clēmēns Melissam (vituperant/vituperāvērunt).

9. The guests **said** 'goodbye'.
   hospitēs 'valē' (dīxērunt/dīcunt).

10. The poet **is walking** in the garden.
    poēta in hortō (ambulat/ambulāvit).

11. Felix **looked for** the baby.
    Fēlīx īnfantem (quaerit/quaesīvit).

12. The slaves **opened** the door.
    servī iānuam (aperuērunt/aperiunt).

© SCAA Enterprises Ltd

7.6 Food for ghosts

Find the English names of two different foods which were left beside tombs as food for the ghosts of the dead.

First fill each set of blanks with a Latin word which translates the English. Then write the numbered letters in the order of their numbers in the spaces provided.

First food offering:

kills   _ _ _₃_ _

nothing   _ _ _ _₆

wine cup   _ _₁_ _ _ _

small   _ _ _ _₇_

suddenly   _ _₄_ _ _

beautiful   _ _ _₂_ _

freedman   _₅_ _ _ _ _ _

Answer: _ _ _ _ _ _ _
        1 2 3 4 5 6 7

Second food offering:

all   _ _ _₄_ _

ghost   _₁_ _ _ _

hits   _ _ _ _₅

however   _ _₂_ _

asks   _ _₃_ _

Answer: _ _ _ _ _
        1 2 3 4 5

© SCAA Enterprises Ltd

7.7 Beliefs about life after death

Study this picture of Roman tombs. Put T (true) or F (false) by the statements below.

1. Look at A. Some tombs looked like small houses. ___
2. Look at B. Tombs like this one would belong to someone very poor. ___
3. Look at C. These tombs lined a road running through the center of the town. ___
4. Look at D. Sometimes tombs and monuments like this were inscribed with messages or greetings to anyone who passed by. ___
5. Some Romans believed that the dead liked to have their possessions with them in the tomb. ___
6. Some families used to hold banquets each year at the tomb to remember the dead relative. ___
7. All Romans took the stories about the underworld very seriously. ___
8. Some Romans agreed with Epicurus that you should enjoy this life fully because there was no afterlife. ___

This Pompeian tombstone gives advice to any human being who passes by – the Latin says *homo* (human, man). You now know enough Latin to work it out. Fill in the English version beside it.

| DUM VIVES, HOMO, BIBE | WHILE ____ ____, MAN, ____ |
| NAM POST MORTEM NIHIL EST | FOR ____ ____ THERE ____ ____ |

© SCAA Enterprises Ltd

8.1 The amphitheater

1 *Look at the plans below. One shows a theater, the other an amphitheater.*

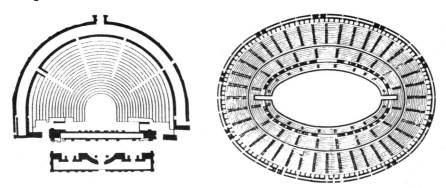

What do you think the prefix **amphi** means in **amphi**theater? **ambi** is another form of the same prefix. What is **amphi** or **ambi** about the following?

a) an **amphibious** animal. _____

b) an **ambiguous** message. _____

c) an **ambidextrous** pupil. _____

2 *Below you will see a list of Latin words connected with the amphitheater. Pair up each word with one from the box below. Then say what is the connection between them. The first one is done for you.*

a) nūntius   nūntiat   nūntius (messenger) nūntiat (announces)

b) bēstia   _____   _____

c) mors   _____   _____

d) pugna   _____   _____

e) clāmor   _____   _____

f) gladiātor _____   _____

| clāmat   nūntiat   bēstiārius   mortuus   pugnat   gladius |

3 Translate this sentence: spectātor spectāculum spectat. _____

_____

Why do the Latin words all start in the same way?

© SCAA Enterprises Ltd

8.2 in amphitheātrō

Translate these sentences, taking care with the tenses.

1. Pompēiānī, postquam amphitheātrum intrāvērunt, bēstiās intentē spectābant.
2. canēs, quod ferōcēs erant, cervōs perterritōs interfēcērunt.
3. postquam lupī canēs facile superāvērunt, spectātōrēs plausērunt.
4. cīvēs erant īrātī quod bēstiāriī leōnēs nōn petīvērunt.
5. cīvēs bēstiāriōs ignāvōs vituperāvērunt quod ex arēnā fugiēbant.

8.3 pāstor et leō

1. *Complete each sentence by using a group of words from the box below. Then translate the sentence into English.*

bēstiās vīdit	eum nōn cōnsūmpsit
quam celerrimē extrāxit	spīnam īnspexit
et eum ad arēnam dūxērunt	

   a) pāstor, quod benignus erat,_____.

   b) pāstor spīnam _____.

   c) Rōmānī hunc pāstōrem comprehendērunt_____
   _____.

   d) pāstor, postquam arēnam intrāvit,_____.

   e) leō, postquam pāstōrem olfēcit,_____.

2. *The Latin word pēs, pedem (foot) gives us many words in English. Write one of these next to the definitions below. The first one is done for you.*

   a) A person who is travelling on **foot**.   pedestrian

   b) A **foot** or base for a statue.   _____

   c) A creature with 100 **feet**.   _____

   d) A creature with 1000 **feet**.   _____

   e) A bicycle part for the **feet**.   _____

   f) Get under someone's **feet**, hinder.   _____

8.4 bēstiae

Complete the following sentences with the correct forms of the words in bold type and then translate the sentences into English.

1 *canis, canem, canēs*

_____ in ātriō sedēbat. amīcus, postquam vīllam intrāvit, _____ salutāvit.

2 *lupus, lupum, lupī, lupōs*

ingēns _____ ululāvit et per silvam festīnāvit.

3 *aper, aprum, aprī, aprōs*

_____ ferōcēs in monte latēbant. iuvenēs _____ saepe agitābant.

4 *cervus, cervum, cervī, cervōs*

_____ arēnam intrāvērunt. gladiātōrēs _____ facile superāvērunt.

5 *leō, leōnem, leōnēs*

_____ lacrimābat quod pēs dolēbat. pāstor _____ audīvit.

6 *serpēns, serpentem, serpentēs*

_____ in pecūniā iacēbat. avārus _____ laudāvit quod servus optimus erat.

7 *pāvō, pāvōnem, pāvōnēs*

_____ in hortō clāmōrem faciēbant. servī _____ audīvērunt.

© SCAA Enterprises Ltd

8.5 Which is the correct accusative?

Look at the first picture. Your teacher will read out two sentences, A and B. Which sentence describes the picture accurately? Put A or B in the box beside the picture. Then do the rest of the exercise in the same way.

© SCAA Enterprises Ltd

8.6 Making a diorama: general instructions

Whatever scene you are making, the basic materials you will need are:

1. A shoe-box. Ask at a shoe store early in the day, before the boxes are crushed and thrown away.
2. Thin, white card – the backs of old birthday cards will do – to make the figures.
3. A thick wad of newspaper to protect the table when you cut the box.
4. Glue.

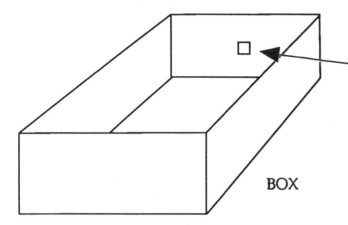
BOX

Cut a viewing-hole about 1.5 cm square, half-way up the short side of the box.

(Make sure, when you put on the lid, that the hole is not covered.)

Cut a window 9 cm x 13 cm. Cut it with the lid this way up, so that you don't break the sides of the lid while cutting.

Cover the window with tracing paper. Glue it to the INSIDE of the lid.

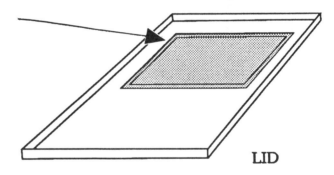
LID

WARNING: Don't cut on the best table. It might be better to ask someone at home to help with cutting the viewing-hole and window, especially if you are using a Stanley knife or similar.

POSITIONING THE FIGURES:
If you put your figures too close to the hole, they will be out of focus. Keep testing the position before you decide where to fix them.

Your diorama will look best if you hold it **under** the electric light so that it shines **down** through the window into the box.

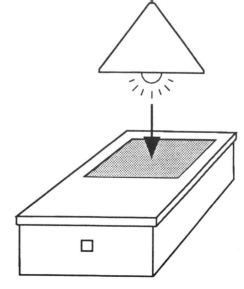

© SCAA Enterprises Ltd

8.6 Making a diorama: Roman amphitheater

This diorama is made in 3 parts, A, B and C. One person could work on A and C, and a partner could do B.

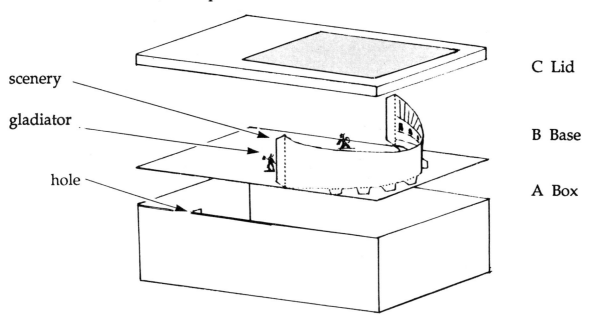

PARTS A AND C
Cut the hole and window by following the general instructions. Ask for help when using craft knives.

PART A
To make the sky you will need pale blue paper (2 sheets of blue duplicating paper would do). Stick this on 3 inside walls of the box (not on the viewing-hole wall, because this wall won't show).

PART B
Cut a flat piece of cardboard, exactly the size of the bottom of the box. This is your base and you will build your scene on this. Color the base a sandy color to imitate the floor of the arena; as an alternative you could use a sheet of sandpaper.

Keep testing to make sure the base fits neatly inside the box. When it is right, take it out of the box to work on.

MAKING THE SCENERY
Color the picture of the amphitheater and cut round the whole thing. Don't cut off the tabs.

Bend the A and B tabs back out of sight. Holding the scenery at both ends, curve it round and test its position on the base. Position the scene towards one end of the base, not the middle. Look at B in the picture above.

Now glue the B tabs to the base. Hold the tabs down firmly until they stick (a second person is useful here).

Don't worry if the sides of the scenery seem to 'flop'. Later you will fix the side tabs to the inside of the box.

© SCAA Enterprises Ltd

8.6 Making a diorama: Roman amphitheater

THE GLADIATORS

Color and stick on thin card *before* you cut round them. Don't cut off the tabs.

Test the best position for the gladiators by looking through the hole. If you put them too near the hole, they will look blurred.

Cut slits in the base and slot the tabs through. Glue the tabs firmly on the underside of the base.

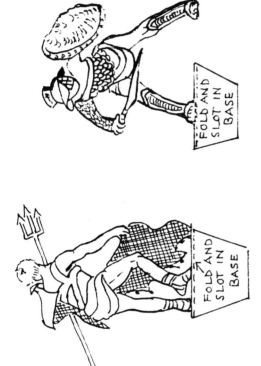

FINAL STAGE

Put some glue in the bottom of the box. Lower the base carefully into the box and press down firmly.

Glue A tabs to the sides of the box.

Put the lid on and hold under an electric light.

ECCE!

© NCC Enterprises Ltd

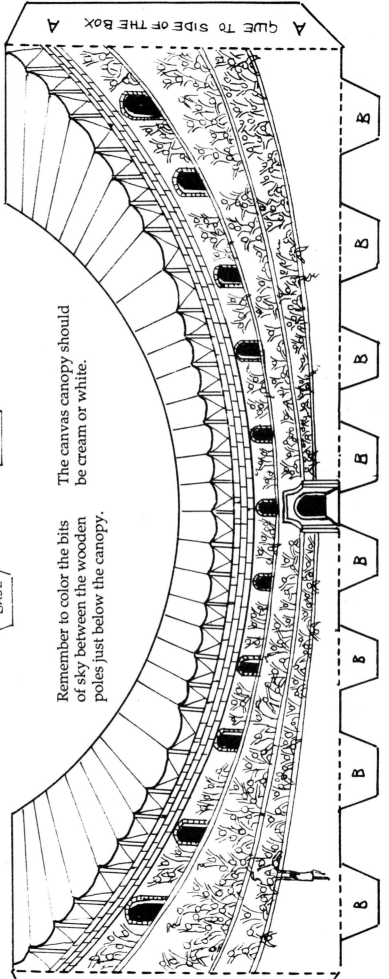

The canvas canopy should be cream or white.

Remember to color the bits of sky between the wooden poles just below the canopy.

9.1 Odd one out

In each set of words circle the one which does not belong.

1. ingēns   parvus   magnus   ferōx
2. caldārium   ātrium   tepidārium   frīgidārium
3. dormiēbat   portābat   contendit   salūtābat
4. cubiculum   sella   lectus   mēnsa
5. clāmat   ululat   pugnat   cantat   lātrat
6. coquus   māter   fīlius   pater   uxor
7. leonine   feline   canine   serpentine   alkaline
8. amīcīs   ancillīs   nūntiōs   mercātōribus   iuvenibus
9. cēnam   hortum   canem   ancillās   vīllam
10. tablīnum   forum   triclīnium   ātrium   cubiculum
11. theātrum   fābula   gladiātor   scaena   āctor
12. mercātor   uxor   tōnsor   āctor   pictor
13. cibus   stola   tunica   toga   ānulus
14. novācula   strigilis   hortus   gladius   stilus
15. puellae   iuvenēs   senēs   fēmina   puerī
16. hortus   forum   palaestra   larārium   peristȳlium
17. fūstis   vīnum   pānis   bibit   cōnsūmit
18. rētiārius   argentārius   murmillō   bēstiārius   gladiātor
19. stābant   sedēbant   servābant   vocant   dūcēbant
20. ignāvus   nūntius   īrātus   benignus   occupātus

9.2 How many words can you find?

1. *Put together as many Latin words as you can, using only the letters in the following sentence:* **discus statuam percussit** (Examples are: tum, discit, pater)

2. Whose statue is this? What is the connection between this statue and the word **ōlim**?

© SCAA Enterprises Ltd

9.3 To whom? For whom?

Look at each picture. Read the sentence and mark the correct word in brackets. Then translate the sentence.

1. Caecilius (Clēmentī, Syphācī) pecūniam dedit.

2. Metella (fīliō, canī) togam quaerēbat.

3. Quīntus (amīcīs, lupīs) fābulam nārrāvit.

4. Caecilius (ancillae, hospitī) vīnum optimum offerēbat.

5. nūntiī (cīvī, cīvibus) spectāculum nūntiāvērunt.

6. leō (pāstōribus, pāstōrī) pedem ostendit.

9.4 in tabernā

Caecilius, Metella and Quintus are going shopping in Pompeii.

1. Find a partner.
2. One of you should play the part of the merchant, the other the part of Caecilius, Metella or Quintus.
3. Choose together ONE thing you want to buy or sell from the box below.

| tunicam | pōculum | statuam | ānulum | stolam | gladium |

4. Read through the dialogue below, putting your article and prices in the gaps. A list of possible prices is given below.
5. Act the dialogue.

Merchant:	salvē! quid quaeris?
Shopper:	salvē, mercātor! ego _____ quaerō.
Merchant:	_____ habeō. ecce!
Shopper:	quantī est?
Merchant:	ego _____ dēnāriōs cupiō.
Shopper:	tū _____ dēnāriōs cupis? furcifer! ego tibi _____ dēnāriōs offerō.
Merchant:	_____ dēnāriōs cupiō.
Shopper:	tibi _____ dēnāriōs offerō.
Merchant:	quid? ego nūllam pecūniam habeō. _____ dēnāriōs cupiō.
Shopper:	tū nimium postulās. ego _____ dēnāriōs dō.
Merchant:	cōnsentiō. ego tibi grātiās maximās agō. valē!

10	decem	35	trīgintā quīnque
15	quīndecim	40	quadrāgintā
20	vīgintī	45	quadrāgintā quīnque
25	vīgintī quīnque	50	quīnquāgintā
30	trīgintā	55	quīnquāgintā quīnque

© SCAA Enterprises Ltd

9.5 in thermīs

1 *The small pictures show different parts of the baths. Write each of the following captions underneath the picture to which it belongs.*

> Pompēiānī sē exercēbant.
> servus dominum rādēbat.
> fēmina ad tabernam ambulābat.
> iuvenis ad thermās vēnit.
> cīvēs togās dēposuērunt.

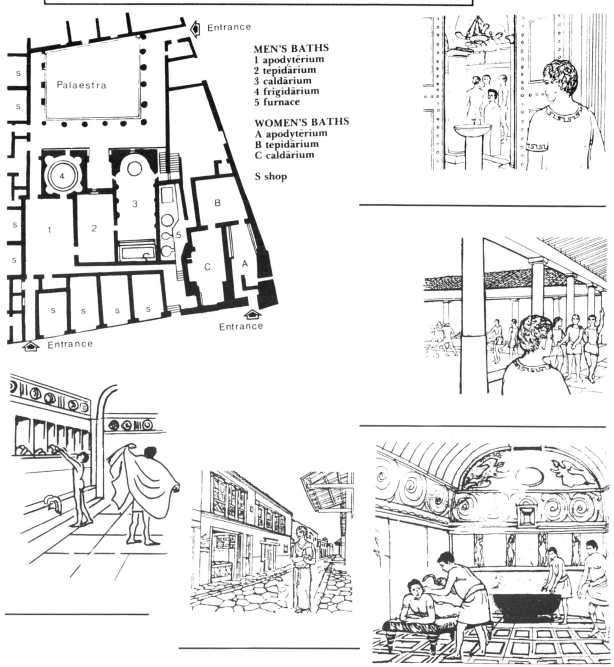

2 *Draw a line from each picture to the right part of the plan.*

© SCAA Enterprises Ltd

9.6 Seneca's noisy neighbors

1   *Seneca wrote about the noise near his lodgings in Rome. Here are some Latin words from his description. As you read through the passage, put the correct letter in the brackets.*

A audiō	B clāmor	C sē exercent	D saliunt
E fūr	F numquam tacet	G habitō	H omnēs

'I am surrounded by uproar ( ). I live ( ) over a set of baths. Just imagine the babel of sounds that strikes my ears. When the **athletic gentlemen** below are exercising themselves ( ), lifting lead weights, I can hear their grunts. I hear ( ) the whistling of their breath as it escapes from their lungs. I can hear somebody enjoying a cheap rub down and the smack of the masseur's hands on his shoulders. If his hand comes down flat, it makes one sound; if it comes down hollowed, it makes another. Add to this the noise of the brawler or **thief** ( ) being arrested down below, the racket made by the man who likes to sing in his bath or the sound of **enthusiasts** who jump ( ) into the water with a tremendous splash. Next, I can hear the screech of the hair-plucker, who advertises himself by shouting. He is never quiet ( ) except when he is plucking hair and making his victim shout instead. Finally, just imagine the cries of the **sausage-man**, the cake-seller, and all ( ) the other food-sellers as they advertise their goods, adding to the din.'

2   *Seneca describes the following people in the baths. Where would they carry on their activities there? Read the passage again for clues and then mark the correct place.*
   a) **athletic gentlemen**: in apodytēriō, in palaestrā, in frīgidāriō
   b) **thief**: in forō, in caldāriō, in apodytēriō
   c) **enthusiasts**: in caldāriō, in cubiculō, in palaestrā
   d) **sausage-man**: in tepidāriō, in triclīniō, in basilicā

3   *Which of these Latin sentences best suits the activities of each individual or group mentioned in 2 above? Put their letter in the bracket.*
   ( ) dis**c**um ēmittēbant   ( ) magnum cl**ā**mōrem faciēbant
   ( ) **c**ibum offerēbat   ( ) togam cēpit et **e**ffūgit

4   *The bold letters in the Latin sentences above make an English word when re-arranged.*
   Clue: it draws hot air up the sides of a room.
   Answer: ___ ___ ___ ___

© SCAA Enterprises Ltd

10.1 What's going on?

Your teacher will read a sentence to you with the verb missed out. Underline the verb which completes the sentence correctly; then translate the whole sentence. The first two have pictures to help you.

1 laudant aedificant vocant _____

2 surgunt cōnsūmunt audiunt _____

3 habitābat vidēbat pulsābat _____

4 contendimus bibimus pingimus _____

5 dedit cōnspexit scrīpsit _____

6 pugnātis lacrimātis intrātis _____

7 terreō ostendō sedeō _____

8 revenīs spectās curris _____

9 habēbat manēbat respondēbat _____

10 intellēxērunt rīsērunt fēcērunt _____

© SCAA Enterprises Ltd

10.2 contentiō

Here is an argument between a Greek (G) and a Roman (R). Complete the sentences with words from the box below. Then, working with a partner, read the sentences as a dialogue.

docēmus	pingimus	estis	aedificāmus	sumus
spectātis	accipitis	audītis	servāmus	facimus
pugnātis	habētis	superāmus	labōrāmus	

R nōs Rōmānī viās et pontēs _____ .

G sed nōs Graecī statuās _____ . nōs pictūrās _____ .

R vōs semper āctōrēs _____ . vōs estis ignāvī. nōs Rōmānī dīligenter _____ .

G vōs estis barbarī quod semper _____ .

R vōs _____ turbulentī quod semper contentiōnēs _____ . nōs Rōmānī pācem _____ .

G sed vōs semper praemium _____ .

R nōs Rōmānī _____ fortissimī. nōs Graecōs semper _____ .

G vōs tamen rhētorēs Graecōs _____ . nōs Graecī Rōmānōs _____ . nōs sumus auctōrēs.

10.3 Make a Roman school report

Make a report card for a boy or girl in Pompeii. If you want to write about a girl, remember she would not attend school beyond the age of fourteen or fifteen.

Remember to include:

  the right type of **teacher** for your pupil's age;

  the right **subjects** for your pupil's age; put in only subjects studied then, not modern ones like Computer Graphics, P.E. etc.;

  any other suitable Roman details – about writing materials, the *paedagōgus* etc.;

  comments on behavior, future career.

You could put grades in Roman numerals, or, if your teacher is Greek, in Greek letters. You could imitate a papyrus scroll.

© SCAA Enterprises Ltd

10.4 Comparisons

Here are some adjectives with their comparatives and superlatives. Pick the most suitable adjectives to complete the Latin captions to the pictures. Look carefully at the three pictures before you choose.

callidus	callidior	callidissimus	longus	longior	longissimus
sordida	sordidior	sordidissima	nōtus	nōtior	nōtissimus
īrātus	īrātior	īrātissimus			

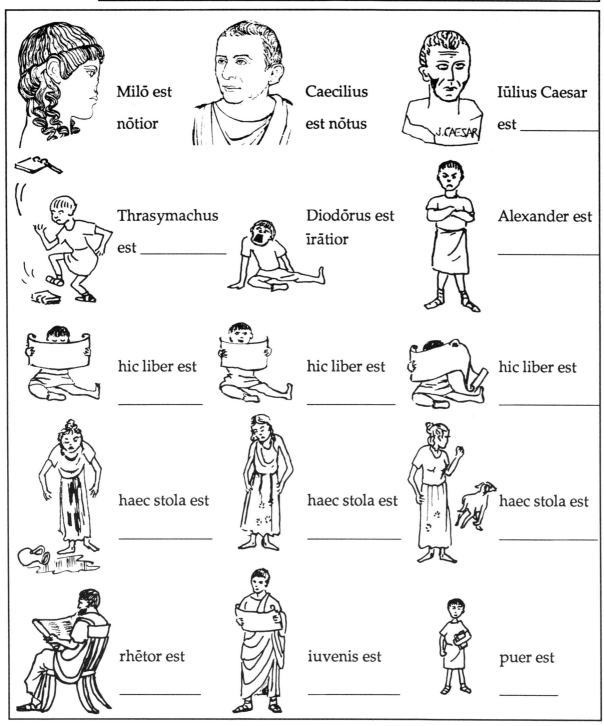

10.5 Teach yourself Greek

Greek was one of the subjects pupils would learn in a Roman school. They would start by learning the letters of the alphabet and their correct pronunciation. Look at the alphabet and see how many letters you recognise and which ones you would have to learn.

Form	Name	English equivalent
Α α	Alpha	a
Β β	Beta	b
Γ γ	Gamma	g (as in **g**ood)
Δ δ	Delta	d
Ε ε	Epsilon	e (as in g**e**t)
Ζ ζ	Zeta	zd (as in wi**sd**om)
Η η	Eta	ē (as in h**ai**r)
Θ θ	Theta	th
Ι ι	Iota	i
Κ κ	Kappa	k
Λ λ	Lambda	l
Μ μ	Mu	m
Ν ν	Nu	n
Ξ ξ	Xi	x
Ο ο	Omicron	o (as in g**o**t)
Π π	Pi	p
Ρ ρ	Rho	r (ῥ = rh)
Σ σ, ς	Sigma	s (ς is used at the end of words)
Τ τ	Tau	t
Υ υ	Upsilon	u
Φ φ	Phi	ph
Χ χ	Chi	ch (as in **ch**orus)
Ψ ψ	Psi	ps
Ω ω	Omega	ō (as in s**aw**)

There is no letter **h** in Greek. To show the sound **h** at the beginning of a word the Greeks used the sign ‘ over a vowel, e.g. ὁδος (a road) pronounced hodos. Words that begin with a vowel but do not have the **h** sound, have the sign ’ over the vowel, e.g. ἐν (in) pronounced en.

© SCAA Enterprises Ltd

10.5 Teach yourself Greek, continued

1 *The following Greek words are still used in English. What are they? You may have to make a few small changes in spelling.*

Greek	English	Greek	English
ΚΟΜΜΑ	_____	δραμα	_____
᾽ΙΡΙΣ	_____	ἠχω	_____
ΚΡΑΤΗΡ	_____	πανθηρ	_____
῾ΟΡΙΖΩΝ	_____	ἀσθμα	_____
ΚΡΙΣΙΣ	_____	νεκταρ	_____
᾽ΙΔΕΑ	_____	ῥοδοδενδρον	_____
ΧΑΟΣ	_____	μανια	_____
ΚΙΝΗΜΑ	_____	ὀρχηστρα	_____
᾽ΑΣΒΕΣΤΟΣ	_____	ἱπποποταμος	_____
ΧΑΡΑΚΤΗΡ	_____	καταστροφη	_____

2 Some of the characters in the stories have Greek names. Look at the list below and write down their names in Latin.

Greek	Latin	Greek	Latin
Μελισσα	_____	Πανταγαθος	_____
Θεοδωρος	_____	῾Ερμογενης	_____
Θρασυμαχος	_____	᾽Αλεξανδρος	_____

Which of these names are still used today in English with little or no change? _____

Here are a few more Greek names that are also used today in English. What are they? Ζωη, Φιλιππος, Δαφνη, ῾Ελενη, Πετρος, Γεωργος

---

3 *The Greek words below were first used in Latin and then came into English. First change the Greek letters into our alphabet, then write down the matching Latin and English words.*

Greek	Our alphabet	Latin word	English word
θεατρον	_____	_____	_____
δισκος	_____	_____	_____
φιλοσοφος	_____	_____	_____
θερμαι	_____	_____	_____
στολη	_____	_____	_____
σκηνη	_____	_____	_____

© SCAA Enterprises Ltd

10.6 Writing materials

What are the writing materials below made of? Choose the right substances from the box below and write them down in the appropriate space below the picture. Some of the articles could be made from more than one substance.

| feather | wax | plastic | reed | aluminum | resin |
| wood | ivory | soot | bronze | stainless steel | bone |

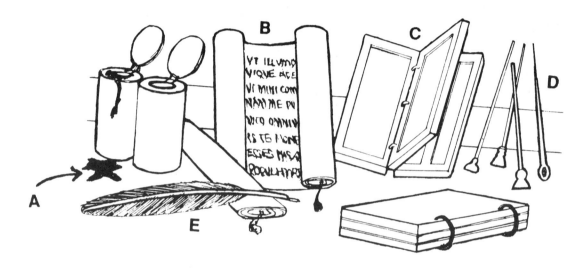

A is made from _____ _____

B is made from _____

C is made from _____ _____

D is made from _____ _____ _____

E is made from _____

What three substances in the box above were not used by the Romans?

_____ _____ _____

Why not? _____

© SCAA Enterprises Ltd

11.1 Questions and answers

Your teacher will read out a series of questions in Latin. Decide which of the people or things below answer each question. Put the question number in the box next to the picture letter.

a) ☐   b) ☐   c) ☐

d) ☐   e) ☐   f) ☐

g) ☐   h) ☐   i) ☐

© SCAA Enterprises Ltd

11.2 Trusting and supporting

Read this conversation and then choose from the right-hand column the correct words which would be used if this story was in Latin. Put the right letter in the bracket.

Clemens	Hello, Poppaea.	
Poppaea	Hello, Clemens. Why are the streets empty today?	
Clemens	All the citizens are in the forum. They are listening to the candidates. My master is giving his support to Holconius ( ).	A Holcōnium B Holcōniō C Holcōnius
Poppaea	My master supports Holconius ( ) too. But Grumio and I support Afer ( ).	A Holcōnius B Holcōnium C Holcōniō A Āfrō B Āfer C Āfrum
Clemens	Afer is a villain! No one trusts Afer ( ).	A Āfer B Āfrō C Āfrum
Poppaea	But Grumio always says 'Afer is a clever candidate.'	
Clemens	Afer is a clever liar. Afer has promised a lot of money to the citizens ( ) but he does nothing.	A cīvēs B cīvibus C cīvem
Poppaea	What does Holconius do? Holconius is an old man and half-asleep! No one supports an old man ( )!	A senex B senem C senī
Clemens	No, Holconius is a generous man. He built a splendid temple for the Pompeians ( ).	A Pompēiānī B Pompēiānīs C Pompēiānōs
Poppaea	But Grumio says …	
Clemens	Grumio is an idiot.	
Poppaea	And you are an idiot too. Goodbye! Grumio is waiting for me near the harbor.	
Clemens	No, Grumio is in the forum. Surely you don't trust Grumio ( )?	A Grumiōnī B Grumiōnem C Grumiō
Poppaea	But Grumio promised … Oh dear, why do I stick up for Grumio ( )? I am very stupid.	A Grumiō B Grumiōnī C Grumiōnem
Clemens	No, you're not stupid, but Grumio is. I'm going back to the house. Are you coming with me?	

11.3 ōrātiō

Read the following election speech and answer the questions.

ego sum Marcus Holcōnius Priscus. ego sum cīvis Rōmānus. gēns mea est nōbilissima. pater meus erat senātor nōtissimus. uxor mea est fidēlis. filiī meī sunt puerī optimī et callidī. amīcī et vīcīnī mihi crēdunt et favent. titulōs in mūrīs cotīdiē scrībunt. ego sum dīves et
5 līberālis. ego Pompēiānīs viās novās prōmittō. ego spectāculum magnificum in amphitheātrō prōmittō. cēterī candidātī sunt mendācēs. vōbīs nihil dant. ego igitur sum līberālior et melior quam omnēs candidātī. dīvīsor fautōribus meīs decem dēnāriōs nunc in forō trādit. mihi favēte, mihi crēdite, ō Pompēiānī!

Words and phrases
vīcīnī   neighbors   cēterī   the rest of

	Points
1 If the candidate did not say that he was a *cīvis Rōmānus* how could we tell?	1
2 *uxor...callidī* (lines 2–3). Why does he include these details about his family?	1
3 What are Holcōnius' friends and neighbors doing to show their support?	2
4 What TWO things does he promise? a) _____ b) _____	2
5 *cēterī...dant* (lines 6–7). What TWO things does Holconius say about the other candidates?	2
6 Underline the sentence which shows that Holconius is offering his supporters bribes. How much is he offering them?	2
7 What does he ask the Pompeians to do at the end of his speech?	1
8 Write down and translate: a) one superlative _____ b) one comparative _____	2
9 Here is a list of adjectives. Mark the ones which Holconius might use to describe himself: dīves nōbilis scelestus caudex mendāx ignāvus benignus stultus probus avārus	2
	15

M·HOLCONIVM PRISCVM·II·VIR

Here is part of one of Holconius' election slogans. What office is he standing for?
Office _____

© SCAA Enterprises Ltd

11.4 Graffiti

These graffiti were found on walls in Pompeii. What do they mean?

1. Aemilius Celer hīc habitat _____
2. Marcus Spedūsa amat _____
3. Nūcerīnīs īnfēlīcia! _____
4. fūr, cavē! _____
5. Minūcī, murmillō, valē! _____
6. Restitūtus multās saepe puellās dēcēpit _____
   _____

7. What does the label below say? _____

   Rūfus est

   Words and phrases
   hīc — here
   īnfēlīcia — bad luck
   Minūcī — Minūcius
   dēcēpit — has deceived

Some of the writers of graffiti made mistakes. Can you find a mistake in the examples above? _____
Choose TWO of the graffiti above and write down who you think wrote them and why.

☐ _____

☐ _____

LABYRINTHVS
HIC HABITAT
MIN   OTAVRVS

This drawing of a maze was also found on a wall in Pompeii. It shows the original style of writing. What does it say?
Clue: There's a monster about!

© SCAA Enterprises Ltd

11.5 Call my bluff

Below are some words that have occurred only once or twice in the Stages. Can you say whether the pictures and descriptions are True (T) or False (F)?

1

2

tepidārium ☐   vēnātiō ☐

3 *aedīlis:* a slave who took his master's children to school. ☐

4 *hypocaust:* a word used by archaeologists to describe burnt objects. ☐

5 *manumission:* the act of making a slave free. ☐

6 *dēnārius:* a gladiator armed with a net and trident. ☐

7 *duovirī:* the officials who judged cases in the basilica. ☐

8 *tabulae:* wax tablets used for notes, letters and wills. ☐

9 *Herculāneum:* the name given to any picture or statue of Hercules. ☐

10 *penātēs:* gods who were thought to protect a Roman household and to look after the store cupboard. ☐

11 *Campānia:* the area in Italy surrounding Pompeii. ☐

12 *peristȳlium:* the exercise ground at the baths. ☐

Can you correct the descriptions you have marked as false?

© SCAA Enterprises Ltd

12.1 The volcano awakes

Look at the pictures and read the questions below them. Choose suitable answers from the box below and put them in the space provided.

minimē   Sulla   ita vērō   in portū   servōs vēndēbat   cinerem

1

ubi erant Syphāx et Celer?
_____

2

cur Syphāx prope portum stābat?
_____

3

num Poppaea et Lucriō erant laetī?
_____

4

quid sēnsit Lucriō?
_____

5
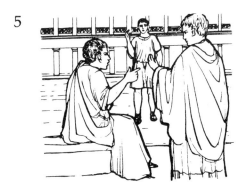
quis ad Marcum et Quārtum contendit?
_____

6

erantne frātrēs sollicitī?
_____

© SCAA Enterprises Ltd

12.2 Which word does not belong?

In each of these groups of words mark the one that is not connected with the word in bold italic type.

1 ***vīlla***
ātrium
tōnsor
culīna
cubiculum
peristȳlium
tablīnum

2 ***cēna***
triclīnium
coquus
larārium
recumbit
bibit
hospes

3 ***Pompēiī***
via
mūrus
portus
taberna
imperium
urbs

4 ***forum***
nāvis
mercātor
statua
argentārius
templum
basilica

5 ***theātrum***
āctor
fābula
gladiātor
spectātor
scaena
plaudit

6 ***servus***
labōrat
līberat
deus
lībertus
vēnālīcius
dominus

7 ***nox***
umbra
lūna
versipellis
stēlla
dormit
canis

8 ***amphitheātrum***
murmillō
arēna
bēstia
stola
pugnat
gladius

9 ***thermae***
fundus
caldārium
palaestra
strigil
apodytērium
togam dēpōnit

10 ***rhētor***
stilus
cibus
cēra
liber
contrōversia
sententia

11 ***candidātus***
duovir
favet
uxor
titulus
scrīptor
crēdit

12 ***mōns Vesūvius***
flamma
cinis
nūbes
sonus
hortus
tremor

© SCAA Enterprises Ltd

12.3 Perfect and imperfect endings

Your teacher will read out a verb in English. Mark the corresponding form in Latin.

1 prōmīsī	prōmīsistī	prōmīsit
2 rapiēbās	rapiēbam	rapiēbat
3 sentiēbat	sentiēbam	sentiēbās
4 pulsāvimus	pulsāvistis	pulsāvērunt
5 īnspiciēbant	īnspiciēbāmus	īnspiciēbātis
6 fugiēbās	fugiēbat	fugiēbam
7 invītāvistis	invītāvērunt	invītāvimus
8 bibī	bibistī	bibit
9 dormīvimus	dormīvērunt	dormīvistis
10 terruistī	terruit	terruī

How many of the words you have marked are in the perfect tense? ☐

How many of the words you have marked are in the imperfect tense? ☐

12.4 Vesuvius

The picture on the left shows Vesuvius as it appears on a wall painting excavated in Pompeii. The other pictures show it as it was after the eruption in A.D. 79 and as it is today. Look at the pictures and describe what has happened to Vesuvius in the last two thousand years.

Before the eruption

After the eruption

Today

12.5 The last days of Pompeii

Complete the account with English words derived from Latin words in the list below. Each one is numbered to help you.

On August 24th A.D. 79 Mount Vesuvius ¹_____ with great ²_____ . The volcano which had lain ³_____ for many years, suddenly awoke. The day before the people had felt earth ⁴_____ and ⁵_____ that disaster was ⁶_____ . Soon the ⁷_____ ⁸_____ were causing ⁹_____ problems and thicker ash was ¹⁰_____ on the town. Some ¹¹_____ in the ¹²_____ and others ¹³_____ as they were trampled by the crowds. Many ¹⁴_____ tried to escape but their hopes were ¹⁵_____ and soon they ¹⁶_____ as buildings collapsed in ¹⁷_____ around them. The ¹⁸_____ scene was one of ¹⁹_____ devastation and the survivors asked themselves whether they were victims of a terrible ²⁰_____ or a punishment from the gods.

1 ērumpit (perfect: ērūpit): breaks out
2 violentia: force
3 dormit: sleeps
4 tremor: shaking
5 sentit (perfect: sēnsit): feels
6 imminet: hangs over, threatens
7 dēnsus: thick
8 fūmus: smoke
9 respīrat: breathes
10 dēscendit: comes down
11 perit: dies
12 flamma: tongue of fire
13 exspīrat: dies
14 obstinātē: stubbornly
15 frūstrā: in vain
16 dēspērat: is without hope
17 ruīna: fallen building
18 fīnis: end
19 tōtus: whole
20 accidit: happens

© SCAA Enterprises Ltd

12.6 Archaeology

Picture D shows a plaster cast of a dog which died in Pompeii during the eruption of Vesuvius in A.D. 79. Many similar casts of people have also been made. Write a sentence about each picture to explain how such a cast was made.

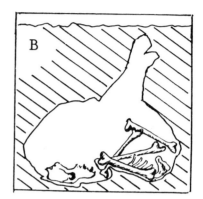
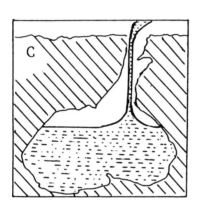
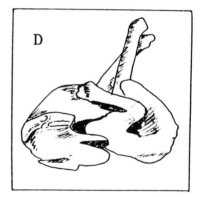

A _____

_____

B _____

_____

C _____

_____

D _____

_____

© SCAA Enterprises Ltd

12.7 The eruption of Vesuvius: an eye-witness account

A young man called Pliny saw the eruption from his uncle's villa at Misenum. His uncle had set out in a boat to rescue some friends near Pompeii. Pliny describes what happened to himself and his mother while they awaited his uncle's return.

The eruption begins

After my uncle set off I spent the rest of the day studying. Then I had a bath, ate my dinner and went to bed. But I didn't get much sleep! We'd been having small earth tremors for some days. They didn't bother us much as we are used to them in Campania, but that night they were bad. Things didn't just shake, they were nearly turned upside-down! I was just getting out of bed to wake my mother when she came bursting into my bedroom to wake me. There's a small courtyard between our house and the sea so we went and sat down there. I don't know whether to call it courage or stupidity – I was only seventeen at the time – but I asked for my book and I carried on reading and taking notes just as if nothing was the matter. Up came a friend of my uncle's who had recently come to stay with him. When he saw us sitting there and me actually reading he told us off – me for being foolhardy and my mother for allowing it. I paid no attention and just carried on reading.

Now it was the first hour of the day and the light was dim and faint. All the buildings around us were tottering and although we were in an open space, it was so narrow that there was every danger that they would crash down on us. In the end we decided to escape from the town.

Chaos

When we'd got clear of the buildings we stopped to get our breath back. There we had some strange and frightening experiences. We had ordered carriages to be brought out for us. They were on dead level ground but even so they kept moving backwards and forwards. We tried wedging stones under their wheels but they wouldn't stay still. Then we saw the sea sucked into itself as if the earthquake had thrown it back. At any rate it had left the sea-bed exposed, and many sea creatures were stranded on the dry sand! Inland there was a terrible black cloud. It was broken by flashing, jagged blasts of flame and yawned open to reveal long tongues of fire. It was like lightning in a thunder cloud – but on a vaster scale.

Then our friend started again in a sharper and more urgent tone. 'If your brother, your uncle is still alive, I'm sure he wants you to be safe. If he's dead, he would want you to survive; so why are you hanging around and not escaping?' We told him that we wouldn't start thinking of our own safety until we knew what had happened to my uncle. He didn't stop to argue but ran away from the danger as fast as his legs would carry him.

12.7 The eruption of Vesuvius: an eye-witness account, continued

It wasn't long before that cloud I've told you about came down to the earth and covered the sea, swallowing up Capreae and blotting out the headland of Misenum. My mother began begging me, urging me, ordering me to escape as best I could. 'You're a young man,' she said. 'You can escape, but I'm old and slow. I don't mind dying – so long as I don't cause your death too.'

I replied that I would not save myself unless she came too. I took hold of her hand and forced her to go forward step by step. She reluctantly agreed and blamed herself for slowing me down.

Darkness

At this point there was a shower of ash, but still not a heavy one. I looked back. Behind us a dense black cloud was getting nearer and nearer.

'Let's get off the road,' I cried, 'while we can still see. Otherwise we'll be knocked down by the crowds following us and get trampled in the darkness.'

We'd hardly found a place to sit when the darkness fell. It wasn't the darkness of a moonless or cloudy night – it was the darkness of an inner room when the lamp goes out. Women were shrieking, babies wailing, men shouting. Children were calling for their parents, parents for their children, wives for their husbands. They were trying to recognize each other by the sound of their voices.

Then there was a glimmer of light, but it wasn't daylight. It was the first flickering of the approaching fire. However, it kept away from us and complete darkness came down again, together with a heavy shower of ash. We had to keep getting up to shake it off; otherwise we would have been buried, crushed under its weight.

The light returns

At last the darkness thinned out and dispersed into smoke and mist. Soon it was real daylight; even the sun broke through, but pale yellow as if it was in eclipse. Still terrified, we saw that everything was changed, buried deep under ash as if under snow. We made our way back to Misenum. There we looked after ourselves as best we could and spent an anxious night wavering between hope and fear. Fear was uppermost as the tremors continued.

But even then, despite the danger we had been through and the danger we saw ahead, we refused to think of escaping until we heard news of my uncle.

© SCAA Enterprises Ltd

12.7 The eruption of Vesuvius: an eye-witness account, continued

Questions

The eruption begins

1. Why did Pliny and his mother not panic when the earth tremors began?
2. Why did they decide to leave the town?

Chaos

3. Pliny describes the effects of the eruption on the land, sea and sky. What were these effects? Why do you think Pliny chooses to write about these particular things?

Darkness

4. To what does Pliny compare the darkness? What idea of the darkness is he trying to give? What effect does the darkness have on the people?
5. What particular dangers threatened Pliny and his mother at this stage of the eruption?

The light returns

6. What reasons have Pliny and his mother still to be worried after the darkness disperses?
7. Look carefully at the map showing the areas affected by falling ash. Does Pliny's account seem to contradict the map?

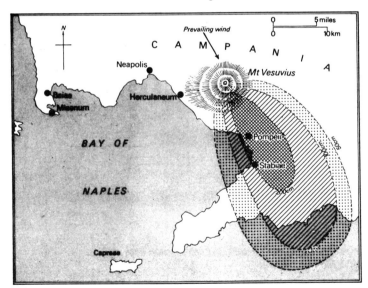

8. Read the whole account again. What impression do you think Pliny wants to give us of:
   a) his uncle's friend   b) his mother   c) himself?
9. What do *you* think of the way they behaved?
10. Pliny wrote this account many years after the eruption. Do you think his description could still be accurate after such a long time? Give your reasons.

© SCAA Enterprises Ltd

12.8 Word search

V	E	S	U	V	I	U	S

Construct your own Latin word search, using the grid provided. Put in only words referring to people or things in the picture above. If you are not sure of a Latin word, look back at the stories and words and phrases list in Stage 12.

Use CAPITAL letters in the grid. Keep a list of the Latin words you have included on a separate sheet. Then try your word search out on a friend.

© SCAA Enterprises Ltd

Teacher's Notes

The exercises are numbered according to the Stage they accompany and their position within the Stage; for example, 1.4 means Stage 1 Exercise 4. The exercises need not be worked through in the order in which they are presented, although the first exercise is often one that can be done early in the Stage.

Where page numbers in the *Cambridge Latin Course* are given, the first number refers to the Third Edition, the one in brackets to the Second Edition which is numbered differently; for example, p.28 (2:10) means page 28 of the Third Edition, which is Stage 2, page 10 in the Second Edition.

Answers are provided for exercises where they are not quickly apparent in the text.

To save paper, exercises may be backed or reduced in size. Students can be asked to write answers in exercise books, thus allowing copies to be re-used. Alternatively, worksheets can be laminated and used with water-soluble pens to enable them to be re-used. Acetate sheets can be used to protect copies in the same way. It is economical to make small sets of such copies and circulate them among groups in the same class. Exercises may also be photocopied on acetate sheets and presented on an overhead projector for oral or written work.

1.1 What does he say? What does he do?

The boxed letters make the following words: 1 pestis; 2 lātrat.

1.2 Where in the house?

This exercise should be done after the background section *Houses in Pompeii* has been studied.

Read aloud the following incomplete sentences to your students and ask them to mark the most likely of the three options on their worksheet. Alternatively, divide the students into pairs. Give one student a copy of the incomplete sentences below and the other a copy of the options. The student with the sentences reads the first four sentences aloud while the other marks the most appropriate option. They then reverse roles and finish the exercise. At the end they compare and discuss the options they have chosen.

Incomplete sentences	Correct choice
1 Caecilius scrībit…	b) in tablīnō
2 coquus labōrat…	a) in culīnā
3 fīlius dormit…	b) in cubiculō
4 servus labōrat…	a) in hortō
5 canis dormit…	b) in viā
6 Quīntus bibit…	c) in triclīniō
7 Metella sedet…	a) in ātriō
8 cibus est…	c) in mēnsā

1.3 What's in a name?

2 The pairs are: i) c); ii) b); iii) f); iv) e); v) a); vi) d)

2.2 Find the hidden sentence

The sentences are:
1 canis in impluviō stat.
2 pater coquum vituperat.
3 canis est pestis.

2.4 amīcus Grumiōnem vīsitat

This is a shorter version of the story in exercise 3 on p.28 (2:10). Read the story in the following sections, pausing after each section. Preface each section with its number.

1 amīcus Grumiōnem vīsitat. amīcus est servus. servus vīllam intrat.

2 Clēmēns est in ātriō.
3 servus Clēmentem videt. Clēmēns servum salūtat.
4 servus culīnam intrat. Grumiō nōn est in culīnā. servus cibum videt.
5 servus cibum gustat. cibus est optimus.
6 Grumiō culīnam intrat. Grumiō amīcum videt. coquus est īrātus. 'pestis! furcifer!' coquus clāmat.

Pictures should be numbered:
left-hand side, starting at the top: 4, 3, 5
right-hand side, starting at the top: 1, 6, 2
Several possible sentences from the longer version in Stage 2 may be used as captions. Younger students may like to cut out, mount and color the pictures. Discuss with them the colors that best convey the materials from which the original artefacts were made, e.g. doors, cooking utensils.

2.6 Roman dinner parties

The references for the translated passages are Martial *Epigrams* XI.52 and Pliny *Letters* I.15.

2.7 More about Roman food

1 The foods and letters (in bold) are a) po*t*atoes; b) cur*r*y; c) c*h*ocolate; d) ba*n*anas; e) t*ea*. The letters when re-arranged make the word *honey*.
2 The missing items are: cherries, sandals, jug, lamp, toga.

3.1 How are these words connected?

This exercise may be done early in the Stage as all the Latin words have occurred in Stages 1 and 2. Students may need help with less familiar words like *laudable* and *dominate*.

3.2 True or false?

Sentences to be read aloud:

			True/False
A	1	Celer est tōnsor.	F
	2	canis est in pictūrā.	F
	3	Celer leōnem pingit.	T
	4	Herculēs est fortis.	T
B	1	ancilla est in tabernā.	F
	2	senex barbam habet.	T
	3	Pantagathus est occupātus.	T
	4	tōnsor barbam tondet.	T
C	1	Caecilius est vēnālīcius.	F
	2	Caecilius servum quaerit.	T
	3	Syphāx prope nāvem stat.	T
	4	vēnālīcius sedet.	F

3.3 Celer, Pantagathus, Syphax

The words connected with the characters are:
Celer: triclīnium, leō, pingit, pictor, pictūra
Pantagathus: tondet, secat, tōnsor, novācula, taberna
Syphāx: emit, vēnālīcius, nāvis, servus, ancilla

3.5 Herculēs et leō

Answers and suggested point scheme:
1	he looks for the lion	1
2	it hears Hercules	1
3	it looks around	1
4	he is brave	1
5	an arrow (1); It doesn't pierce the lion's skin/the lion's skin is too tough (1)	2
6	unhappy/disheartened (1); ēheu (1)	2
7	a club	1
8	it has beaten off Hercules' attack/it thinks it can win or similar	1
9	pestis! furcifer!/pest! scoundrel!	1
10	he strangles it	1

The twelve labors were:
1. killing the Nemean lion
2. killing the Lernaean hydra
3. capturing the Ceryneian hind with the golden horns
4. capturing the Erymanthean boar
5. cleaning the Augean stables
6. killing the Stymphalian birds
7. capturing the Cretan bull
8. obtaining the mares of Diomedes
9. obtaining the girdle of Hippolyta, queen of the Amazons
10. killing the three-bodied monster, Geryon
11. obtaining apples from the garden of the Hesperides
12. bringing up Cerberus from the Underworld

3.6 In Pompeii

It may be helpful for students to revise their knowledge of Pompeii by studying the plan on p.43 (3:13) of their textbook before embarking on this exercise. After completing it, students could be asked to make up similar couplets for a quiz on the Pompeian villa or other aspects of Pompeii.

Answers: E L N S I P O A

The letters when rearranged make the word Neapolis, modern Naples.

4.1 Who am I?

This exercise may be done early in the Stage after the Model Sentences, as its vocabulary is taken from earlier Stages. It lends itself to oral work and may be done twice: the first time with occupations, the second with names.

Students may need help with accusative and verb forms when making up their own sentences at the end.

4.3 A day in court

The complete text is:

After the judge entered the *basilica/law court* he asked Caecilius' name. Then he wanted to know if Caecilius was a *Pompeian/citizen of Pompeii* and what he did in the *city*. Caecilius told the judge that he was a *banker* and that he came to the *forum* every day. He said that he was bringing a charge against *Hermogenes* who owed him *a lot of money* and had not *returned* it. Suddenly someone shouted that Caecilius was a *liar*. The judge did not like the interruption and asked *'Who are you?'* The man replied,*'I am Hermogenes.'* When the judge asked him what he was doing in the *city*, he replied that he was a *merchant* and was doing business in the *forum*. Then the judge asked if he owed *money*. Hermogenes replied that he *did not owe money* and that he had a friend who was a *witness*. Hermogenes' friend claimed that *Hermogenes* did not *owe money* and that *Caecilius* was a liar. This made Caecilius so angry that he shouted out that *Hermogenes* was a liar and so was his *friend*. The judge interrupted and said that Caecilius had to *prove* his case. Caecilius said that he had a *wax tablet* and that the judge could *see* Hermogenes' *seal* in the wax. *Hermogenes* groaned and the judge asked him if he had a *ring*. Caecilius told the judge that Hermogenes was *hiding* his ring. The judge demanded the *ring* and announced that it *proved* the case. Then the *judge* convicted Hermogenes.

4.4 forum or basilica?

forum: taberna; emit; tōnsor; vēndit; argentāria
basilica: testis; iūdex; accūsat; convincit; rem nōn probat

4.5 How is Latin pronounced?

Answers: 1 material; 2 high; 3 sad; 4 let; 5 put; 6 corner; 7 red door; 8 gag; 9 wonder

4.6 Finding your way round the forum

Students may need to be referred to the plan of the forum on p.63 (4:14) to get their bearings.

Answers: 1 A; 2 O; 3 R; 4 D; 5 E; 6 F; 7 V; 8 U; 9 N; 10 M; 11 T; 12 I.

The sentence at the end should read: *Caecilius ad forum venit.*

5.1 Compliments or insults?

The Latin words on which this exercise is based have occurred in Stage 4 or earlier. This is a demanding exercise and students may require help from the teacher or a dictionary.

5.2 Singular or plural?

This is a very straightforward exercise, suitable for less able students. Read aloud the following sentences, with their numbers. The corresponding picture letter is given in brackets.

1	canis est in viā.	(E)
2	servī sunt in viā.	(G)
3	puerī sunt in viā.	(H)
4	fēmina est in viā.	(F)
5	puer est in viā.	(B)
6	canēs sunt in viā.	(A)
7	fēminae sunt in viā.	(C)
8	servus est in viā.	(D)

5.4 Find the hidden sentence

The sentences are:
1. nūntius in forō clāmat.
2. Pompēiānī ad urbem contendunt.
3. senex in theātrō dormit.
4. servus in vīllā manet.

5.5 in theātrō

Answers:
1. C B A
3. The sentence at the end should read: ĀCTOR IN SCAENĀ STAT.

5.6 and 5.7 The Ghost / Theatrical masks

The masks are of the characters in the scene from the Mostellaria in 5.6. A summary of the plot of the play is given in the textbook p.82 (5:15).

Students may also enjoy acting the play *Poppaea* in Stage 5, which has some of the flavor of Roman comedy. The masks in 5.7 could be used for Lucrio and Grumio; Poppaea's mask might be modelled on that of the figurine of the masked girl in Stage 10.

6.1 pugna

This exercise may be done after the first story, *pugna*, has been read. All the vocabulary is taken from the story or the Model Sentences.

6.2 After or because?

This exercise uses familiar vocabulary, but students should be handling *postquam* and *quod* clauses well before it is attempted.

The sentences are:

1. amīcī, *quod cēna erat optima*, coquum laudābant.
2. agricolae, *quod erant īrātī*, mercātōrem pulsābant.
3. iūdex, *postquam ānulum spectāvit*, Hermogenem vituperāvit.
4. Pompēiānī, *postquam fābulam spectāvērunt*, āctōrēs laudāvērunt.
5. Caecilius, *postquam tabernam intrāvit*, vīnum gustāvit.
6. servus, *quod dominus dormiēbat*, nōn labōrābat.

6.3 poēta et canis

This simple story, designed to consolidate the imperfect and perfect tenses, is suitable for less able students.

6.4 What did they do?

Read aloud the following incomplete sentences and leave time for students to write their translations. With average or weak students, it would be more helpful to do the exercise in three stages: first read the incomplete sentences and ask students to select the right verb; then check their answers; finally, read the correct complete sentences aloud and ask students to write down the translation.

Incomplete sentences	Correct verbs
1 Caecilius pecūniam…	numerāvit
2 fēminae per viam…	ambulābant
3 spectātōrēs in theātrō…	sedēbant
4 vēnālīcius ancillās…	vēndēbat
5 poēta versum…	recitāvit
6 mercātor agricolam…	pulsāvit
7 servī in vīllā…	labōrābant
8 amīcī ad forum…	festīnāvērunt

6.5 The life of a slave

The game, which will take only a few minutes, should be followed by the written or oral work suggested on the student's worksheet.

7.1 What do you see in the picture?

This exercise may be done early in the Stage, after the Model Sentences have been read.

7.2 fābula mīrābilis

This oral exercise will help to consolidate the events and language of the story. Remember to read the letter before each sentence.

The sentences are:

    A ingēns lupus subitō appāruit.
    B tunica lapidea in viā iacēbat.
    C amīcus valdē timēbat.
    D lūna in caelō lūcēbat.
    E prope viam erat silva.

The correct sequence of letters starting at the middle left and proceeding clockwise is A D E C B.

7.3 The wasp

A very simple story, practicing sentences with the subject omitted.

7.4 Night horror

The paired words are:

appāret	apparition
terret	terrifying/terrible/terror
cautē	cautiously
mortuus	mortal
sōlus	solitary
dēsertus	deserted
pulsat	pulse
obscūrus	obscured
vīta	vital
agricola	agricultural
nox, noctem	nocturnal
horribilis	horror/horrible
habitat	inhabitant
īnsānus	insane

7.6 Food for ghosts

This exercise consolidates vocabulary in the checklists for Stages 6 and 7. The foods are lentils and beans.

7.7 Beliefs about life after death

Answers: 1T; 2F; 3F; 4T; 5T; 6T; 7F; 8T

8.1 The amphitheater

This exercise may be used after *vēnātiō* has been read.

1. Students may need help with this question unless they are able to consult dictionaries. The simplest explanation is to say that amphi- and ambi- mean 'on both sides', 'double' or 'two'. Therefore:

    a) amphibious = able to live both on land and in water
    b) ambiguous = having a double/two meanings
    c) ambidextrous = able to use both hands equally well.

8.3 pāstor et leō

The complete sentences are:

a) pāstor, quod benignus erat, *spīnam īnspexit*.
b) pāstor spīnam *quam celerrimē extrāxit*.
c) Rōmānī hunc pāstōrem comprehendērunt *et eum ad arēnam dūxērunt*.
d) pāstor, postquam arēnam intrāvit, *bēstiās vīdit*.
e) leō, postquam pāstōrem olfēcit, *eum nōn cōnsūmpsit*.

8.5 Which is the correct accusative?

The sentences are:

1. A Metella amīcum vocāvit.
   B Metella amīcōs vocāvit.
2. A cīvēs nūntiōs audiēbant.
   B cīvēs nūntium audiēbant.
3. A gladiātōrēs Pompēiānum salūtāvērunt.
   B gladiātōrēs Pompēiānōs salūtāvērunt.
4. A Grumiō cēnam portāvit.
   B Grumiō cēnās portāvit.
5. A spectātōrēs āctōrem spectāvērunt.
   B spectātōrēs āctōrēs spectāvērunt.
6. A amīcus iuvenēs laudāvit.
   B amīcus iuvenem laudāvit.
7. A Quīntus canēs pulsāvit.
   B Quīntus canem pulsāvit.
8. A vēnālīcius ancillās vēndēbat.
   B vēnālīcius ancillam vēndēbat.

The correct choices are: 1A; 2A; 3B; 4A; 5B; 6B; 7B; 8A.

8.6 Making a diorama

All three sheets are required for this activity.

Roman houses, baths, the forum and the theater also make good dioramas.

9.1 Odd one out

Answers:

1	ferōx	11	gladiātor
2	ātrium	12	uxor
3	contendit	13	cibus
4	cubiculum	14	hortus
5	pugnat	15	fēmina
6	coquus	16	larārium
7	alkaline	17	fūstis
8	nūntiōs	18	argentārius
9	ancillās	19	vocant
10	forum	20	nūntius

9.2 How many words can you find?

2 Answer: Milō (ōlim is Milō backwards)

9.3 To whom? For whom?

Correct choices in 1–4 depend on sense criteria, those in 5 and 6 on the distinction between dative singular and plural.

9.4 in tabernā

This dialogue is closely based on the story *in tabernā*. Teachers may have to respond to requests for dressing up or producing objects.

9.5 in thermīs

Captions should read, clockwise from top right:

iuvenis ad thermās vēnit.

Pompēiānī sē exercēbant.

servus dominum rādēbat.

fēmina ad tabernam ambulābat.

cīvēs togās dēposuērunt.

The parts of the baths shown in the pictures, clockwise from top right, are: entrance, palaestra, caldārium, shop, apodytērium.

9.6 Seneca's noisy neighbors

Answers:

1 B G C A E D F H
2 a) **athletic gentlemen:** in palaestrā
   b) **thief:** in apodytēriō
   c) **enthusiasts:** in caldāriō
   d) **sausage-man:** in tepidāriō
3 a) disc*um* ēmittēbant
   d) cibum of*fer*ēbat
   c) magnum c*lām*ōrem faciēbant
   b) togam cēpit et *ef*fūgit
3 Answer: **flue.** Some students may not know this word. It does, however, occur in the background section of Stage 9, p.148 (9:15) last line and in the plan of a hypocaust on the following page.

10.1 What's going on?

This exercise may be used after *contrōversia* has been read. Read aloud the following incomplete sentences and leave time for students to write their translations. As an alternative for less able students read the sentences one by one to enable students to select the right verb; then check their answers; as a final exercise read the correct version of each sentence aloud and pause while students write down their translation.

	Incomplete sentences	Correct verbs
1	architectī viās et pontēs…	aedificant
2	iuvenēs rhētorem in palaestrā…	audiunt
3	pictor Graecus prope forum…	habitābat
4	nōs pictōrēs pictūrās optimās…	pingimus
5	Quīntus amīcō dōnum splendidum…	dedit
6	vōs barbarī ferōciter…	pugnātis
7	ego Quīntō discum…	ostendō
8	tū āctōrēs in theātrō…	spectās
9	agricola fundum prope urbem…	habēbat
10	sculptōrēs Graecī statuās pulchrās…	fēcērunt

10.2 contentiō

The vocabulary of this exercise is taken mainly from the Model Sentences and from *contrōversia*. Pupils may need help with the words *praemium* and *accipitis* which occur once in *statuae*.

R nōs Rōmānī viās et pontēs *aedificāmus*.

G sed nōs Graecī statuās *facimus*. nōs pictūrās *pingimus*.

R vōs semper āctōrēs *spectātis*. vōs estis ignāvī. nōs Rōmānī dīligenter *labōrāmus*.

G vōs estis barbarī quod semper *pugnātis*.

R vōs *estis* turbulentī quod semper contentiōnēs *habētis*. nōs Rōmānī pācem *servāmus*.

G sed vōs semper praemium *accipitis*.

R nōs Rōmānī *sumus* fortissimī. nōs Graecōs semper *superāmus*.

G vōs tamen rhētorēs Graecōs *audītis*. nōs Graecī Rōmānōs *docēmus*. nōs sumus auctōrēs.

10.5 Teach yourself Greek

Explanations about the Greek alphabet have been kept to a minimum.

Second sheet

1. Accents have been omitted for the sake of simplicity. Students may need help with some of the English meanings; they could be referred to dictionaries, if available.

2. Students might be asked why these particular characters had Greek names. Possible explanations:

   Melissa came from Greece or the Greek-speaking East;

   Thrasymachus and his brother Alexander may have been descended from one of the original Greek colonizing families or from more recent commercial immigrants;

   Theodorus was probably a native Greek speaker, perhaps a Greek freedman, like many teachers;

   Hermogenes was a Greek merchant with a boat trading between Greece and Italy;

   there are no clues about the history of the barber Pantagathus; perhaps he was a Greek freedman, set up in business by his previous master.

   Students might also be asked how they could guess that some names are Greek in origin, e.g. Theodorus, Thrasymachus, Philippus. They might realise that *th, ch* and *ph* are transliterations of the Greek double letters θ, χ and φ.

   Students may not be familiar with the name Theodore, but will certainly recognize Melissa and Alexander.

3. Students may need help with English *therm, thermal, stole* and *scene,* and with Latin *scaena.*

10.6 Writing materials

Answers:

A soot, resin
B reed
C wood, wax
D ivory, bone, bronze
E feather

Substances not used by the Romans: stainless steel, plastic, aluminum.

Why not? The processes of making them were not known in Roman times.

11.1 Questions and answers

This exercise may be done after the first story has been read. Read out the following questions, with their numbers. With less able students it would be advisable to check that they understand the question format before they begin.

Questions	Picture letter
1 quid facit sculptor?	c)
2 quid pingit pictor?	d)
3 quid in mūrō scrībit scrīptor?	i)
4 quid aedificat architectus?	f)
5 quid portant rhētorēs?	b)
6 quid vēndunt vēnālīciī?	a)
7 quid habet argentārius?	g)
8 quid in tabernā habet caupō?	h)
9 quid gerit cīvis Rōmānus?	e)

More able students may also be able to supply appropriate Latin words to complete the sentences.

11.2 Trusting and supporting

This exercise is best done after the play, as it refers to Poppaea's relationship with Clemens and Grumio in the last scene. It may be helpful to emphasize that *crēdō* and *faveō* are used with the dative in Latin, whatever their translations in English, e.g. in the sentence 'But Grumio and I support Afer,' Afer will be in the dative case in Latin.

Answers: B: Holcōniō; C: Holcōniō; A: Āfrō; B: Āfrō; B: cīvibus; C: senī; B: Pompēiānīs; A: Grumiōnī; B: Grumiōnī

Able students might be asked to translate the whole dialogue into Latin. This would take very little time if the parts were distributed to individuals or pairs for translation.

11.3 ōrātiō

Answers and suggested point scheme:
1. his three names/his father was a senator — 1
2. to make people think he is a good husband and father **or similar** — 1
3. writing slogans on walls (every day) — 2
4. a) new roads (1) (b) magnificent show in amphitheater (1) — 2
5. they are liars (1) they don't give the Pompeians anything (1) — 2
6. dīvīsor...trādit (1) decem dēnāriōs/10 denarii (1) — 2
7. support and trust him — 1
8. one of:
   nōbilissima: very noble (1)
   nōtissimus: very famous (1)
   optimī: very good (1)
   one of:
   līberālior: more generous (1)
   melior: better (1) — 2
9. dīves, nōbilis, benignus, probus (½ each) — 2

As an additional exercise, students might adopt the role of a Pompeian candidate and make up their own election speech in English. A mock election would be a popular activity.

11.4 Graffiti

Translations:
1. Aemilius Celer lives here.
2. Marcus loves Spedusa.
3. Down with the Nucerini! A reference to the enmity between the Pompeians and the Nucerini which culminated in the riot in the amphitheater in A.D. 59.
4. Thief, beware!
5. Goodbye, Minucius the murmillo!
6. Restitutus has often deceived many girls.
7. It's Rufus.

Mistake: Spedūsa for Spedūsam.

The labyrinth. Here lives the Minotaur.

11.5 Call my bluff

Answers: 1F 2T 3F 4F 5T 6F 7T
8T 9F 10T 11T 12F

12.1 The volcano awakes

This simple exercise based on the Model Sentences is suitable for less able students.

Answers:
1 in portū   4 cinerem
2 servōs vēndēbat   5 Sulla
3 minimē   6 ita vērō

Some teachers may wish students to answer in complete sentences. This exercise could easily be adapted to an oral exercise, if the questions were deleted from the student's sheet and the directions changed.

12.2 Which word does not belong?

Answers:
1. tōnsor
2. larārium
3. imperium
4. nāvis
5. gladiātor
6. deus
7. canis
8. stola
9. fundus
10. cibus
11. uxor
12. hortus

12.3 Perfect and imperfect endings

Read out the following English verbs, with their numbers.

English verbs	Answers
1 I promised	prōmīsī
2 I was grabbing	rapiēbam
3 you were feeling	sentiēbās
4 you punched	pulsāvistis
5 we were inspecting	īnspiciēbāmus
6 you were running away	fugiēbās
7 they invited	invītāvērunt
8 I drank	bibī
9 they slept	dormīvērunt
10 she frightened	terruit

Number of verbs in perfect tense, 6; in imperfect tense, 4.

12.4 Vesuvius

Until A.D. 79 Vesuvius was cone-shaped; in A.D. 79, the top of the mountain was blown off, leaving an enormous crater. Since then a new cone has formed. There have been several eruptions since, the most recent being the serious eruption of 1944.

12.5 The last days of Pompeii

Answers:
1. erupted
2. violence
3. dormant
4. tremors
5. sensed
6. imminent
7. dense
8. fumes
9. respiratory
10. descending
11. perished
12. flames
13. expired
14. obstinately
15. frustrated
16. were in despair; despaired
17. ruins
18. final
19. total
20. accident

12.6 Archaeology

The process is explained in Stage 12, p.199 (12:15).

12.7 The eruption of Vesuvius: an eye-witness account

Notes on the last two questions:

9 If students are inclined to accept the heroism of Pliny and his mother and the cowardice of his uncle's friend without question, the teacher could perhaps put a contrary view. There is a good discussion in Unit 4 Teacher's Manual, p.158.

10 It was Pliny's habit to make notes as he was indeed doing at the beginning of the eruption; he was no doubt influenced by the example of his uncle whose constant note-taking he records in a letter. It is therefore likely that he kept careful and detailed notes of his experience of the eruption. As the eruption was such a catastrophic event he may well have had the events indelibly imprinted on his memory. Observations of later eruptions confirm many of the details described by Pliny.